Social Attitudes in Northern Ireland

SOCIAL ATTITUDES IN NORTHERN IRELAND

The Ninth Report

Edited by

Katrina Lloyd, Paula Devine, Ann Marie Gray
and Deirdre Heenan

Pluto Press

LONDON • STERLING, VIRGINIA

First published 2004 by Pluto Press
345 Archway Road, London N6 5AA
22883 Quicksilver Drive, Sterling, VA 20166-2012, USA

Distributed in the Republic of Ireland and Northern Ireland by
Columba Mercier Distribution, 55A Spruce Avenue, Stillorgan Industrial Park,
Blackrock, Co. Dublin, Ireland. Tel: +353 1 294 2556. Fax: +353 1 294 2564

www.plutobooks.com

British Library Cataloguing in Publication Data
A catalogue record for this book is available from the British Library

ISBN 0 7453 2156 9 hardback

Library of Congress Cataloging in Publication Data applied for

10 9 8 7 6 5 4 3 2 1

Designed and produced for Pluto Press by
Chase Publishing Services, Fortescue, Sidmouth, EX10 9QG, England
Typeset from disk by Newgen Imaging Systems (P) Ltd., India
Printed and bound in the European Union by
Antony Rowe Ltd, Chippenham and Eastbourne, England

Contents

List of Tables

Introduction

Katrina Lloyd, Paula Devine, Ann Marie Gray
and Deirdre Heenan

This is the ninth volume in a series on social attitudes in Northern Ireland. Seven of the eight previous editions (Stringer and Robinson, 1991, 1992; 1993; Breen, Devine and Robinson, 1995; Breen, Devine and Dowds, 1996; Dowds, Devine and Breen, 1997; Robinson, Heenan, Gray and Thompson, 1998) were based on data from the Northern Ireland Social Attitudes (NISA) survey series. The eighth volume (Gray, Lloyd, Devine, Robinson and Heenan, 2002) and this volume are based on the successor to that survey – the Northern Ireland Life and Times survey.

Since 1989, these attitudinal surveys and the output from them – both in the edited volumes and the on-line Research Updates <http://www.ark. ac.uk/publications/updates> – have become an acknowledged source of information on contemporary values in Northern Ireland. This volume, drawing largely on data collected in the 2000 and 2001 Life and Times surveys, includes a broad spectrum of policy-relevant chapters from an authoritative list of Northern Ireland commentators, which includes academics and those who are involved in informing policy-making within the community. A number of important issues are explored in the chapters in this volume. These include the extent of change in attitudes centred on religion, politics and community relations. These issues are, of course, omnipresent in any debate on Northern Ireland, and the Life and Times survey is committed to ensuring reliable monitoring of them, especially in the current volatile political environment. In addition to these core time-series areas, which are unique to Northern Ireland, other topics explored in this volume contribute to the more general social policy debate and include health, social capital, lifelong learning, men's issues, culture and attitudes to work. As with previous volumes in the series, in all the chapters in this volume the distinctive features of Northern Ireland social policy form a backdrop to a detailed examination of the issues. In some cases, comparisons are made with Britain, as well as with findings from earlier years of NISA and the Life and Times survey.

The Life and Times survey was launched in the autumn of 1998. Its mission is to monitor the attitudes and behaviour of people in Northern Ireland to a range of social policy issues. By running annually, the survey provides a time series and a public record of how attitudes and behaviours in Northern Ireland develop across the years.

In particular, the survey aims to provide:

- a local resource for use by the general public, and
- a data source for a more theoretical academic debate.

The Life and Times survey is a direct descendent of the NISA survey which ran from 1989 to 1996. NISA was a sister survey to the British Social Attitudes (BSA) survey and, by running the same modules as the BSA, it provided a time series of social attitudes, and allowed comparisons with Britain. When funding for NISA ended in 1996, the opportunity was taken to develop a new survey that would continue to record attitudes to social policy issues in Northern Ireland, but would cut the close link to the BSA to allow for a more specific emphasis on Northern Ireland. Therefore, the main focus of the Life and Times survey is on Northern Irish social policy issues. While the Life and Times survey is designed to be used by the wider public in Northern Ireland, it is also intended for use by anyone with an interest in social policy issues in Northern Ireland and elsewhere. To this end, each year's survey includes a substantial component that either continues an old NISA time series, or replicates a BSA module.

In addition, since 1989, Northern Ireland has taken part in the International Social Survey Programme (ISSP) via NISA, and now via the Life and Times survey. Every year, 38 countries participate in this programme in which the same module of questions is asked cross-nationally. This enables comparison with findings from a diverse range of countries. Individual datasets for all the member countries can be obtained from the Zentralarchiv für Empirische Sozialforschung (Central Archive for Empirical Social Research) at the University of Cologne, Germany, which is the official archive of the ISSP. The Zentralarchiv also produces a merged datafile for each year, containing data from all countries. Information on the ISSP can be found at its web site at <http://www.issp.org>, while the English version of the Zentralarchiv web site is at <http://www.gesis.org/en/za/index.htm>.

The fact that this volume is possible is due to the many generous funders who have supported the Life and Times survey since its inception. We are grateful to those who funded modules in the 2000 and 2001 Life and Times surveys, which have been used to produce this volume. These include the Central Community Relations Unit (now the Equality Unit Research Branch within the Office of the First Minister and Deputy First Minister), which has supported a module focusing on community relations each year since 1989. The chapter by Harbison and Manwah Lo in this volume shows the benefits of such a time series. Other government departments that have supported modules in the 2000 and 2001 surveys include the Department for Social Development and the Department of Culture, Arts and Leisure. The BUPA Foundation provided funding for the module on Health Issues while support was also forthcoming from Queen's University Belfast and the University of Ulster. The Nuffield Foundation has also provided continuous support through its on-going interest in education in Northern Ireland and funded the module on Education in the 2001 survey. The Economic and Social Research Council has demonstrated its interest in Northern Ireland matters through support for the Political Attitudes module in 2001 under its 'Devolution and Constitutional Change' Programme (Award Number: L219252024).

Finally, this survey is quite unique in that it is a genuine collaboration between the two universities in Northern Ireland – the University of Ulster and Queen's University Belfast. Both institutions have provided invaluable financial and practical support to the survey, and the editors and survey team wish to record their sincere appreciation of this support.

The Life and Times series is, of course, a team effort. In particular, the survey coordinator, Lizanne Dowds, deserves special mention for her vision and enterprise in establishing and continuing to develop the survey. The survey team is also supported by Research and Evaluation Services, which has conducted the fieldwork since 1998. We are grateful to Peter Ward and his team for the continuation of its efficient service.

The Life and Times survey is conducted each year in the hope that its findings may impact positively upon policy-making in the region. We reserve our warmest appreciation for all of those anonymous respondents to the survey who give freely of their time. Without them, no research of this kind is possible. We hope you will find the results of interest and may indeed benefit in some small way from the findings. For more information on all aspects of the Life and Times survey, please visit our web site at <http://www.ark.ac.uk/nilt>. Life and Times is a constituent part of ARK – the Northern Ireland Social and Political Archive <http://www.ark.ac.uk>.

REFERENCES

Breen, R., Devine, P. and Dowds, L. (eds) (1996) *Social Attitudes in Northern Ireland: The Fifth Report, 1995–1996* (Belfast: Appletree Press).

Breen, R., Devine, P. and Robinson, G. (eds) (1995) *Social Attitudes in Northern Ireland: The Fourth Report, 1994–1995* (Belfast: Appletree Press).

Dowds, L., Devine, P. and Breen, R. (eds) (1997) *Social Attitudes in Northern Ireland: The Sixth Report, 1996–1997* (Belfast: Appletree Press).

Gray, A.M., Lloyd, K., Devine P., Robinson, G. and Heenan, D. (eds) (2002) *Social Attitudes in Northern Ireland: The Eighth Report* (London: Pluto Press).

Robinson, G., Heenan, D., Gray, A.M. and Thompson, K. (eds) (1998) *Social Attitudes in Northern Ireland: The Seventh Report* (Aldershot: Ashgate).

Stringer, P. and Robinson, G. (eds) (1991) *Social Attitudes in Northern Ireland, 1990–91 Edition* (Belfast: Blackstaff Press).

Stringer, P. and Robinson, G. (eds) (1992) *Social Attitudes in Northern Ireland: The Second Report, 1991–92* (Belfast: Blackstaff Press).

Stringer, P. and Robinson, G. (eds) (1993) *Social Attitudes in Northern Ireland: The Third Report, 1992–1993* (Belfast: Blackstaff Press).

1
Cinderfella (Finally) Goes to the Ball

Colin Fowler and Paula Devine

ONCE UPON A TIME ... THE CONTEXT OF MEN'S ISSUES
AND WORK IN NORTHERN IRELAND

The invisible man

If we were to organise a street survey – wherein we asked passers-by to describe what 'women's issues' are – it's very likely that most people would probably make a reasonably good attempt at it. Yet, at the same time, many people still find it very difficult to comprehend what 'men's issues' are, what they might include or, indeed, why we should even pose this question in the first place. This, in itself, is bad enough. However, the problem is accentuated and compounded because it is also extremely difficult to access substantive, scientifically rigorous, academic research into local males' needs, issues, values, attitudes and life experiences. The Invisible Man is not, therefore, just a creation of H.G. Wells' overly active imagination.

Despite the 2001 Census figures telling us that there are 821,449 males in Northern Ireland – constituting 48.74 per cent of the population (Northern Ireland Statistics and Research Agency, 2002) – the world of local men and boys is still, definitely, at the edge of our understanding. At best, we make assumptions about their views and, at worst, we rely on stereotypes that are passed from one generation to the next. In the absence of a body of empirical data, we end up increasing our understanding of male attitudes and values by evaluating the actions of cartoon characters, such as Homer and Bart Simpson. Of course, this is funny – even insightful – but it is hardly a solid basis for future policy and service development!

Until now, there has never been a large-scale random sample survey of attitudes and values to a range of men's issues conducted within Northern Ireland – except by commercial companies eager to increase their sales of cars, beer, mobile phones or the like. Men's Life and Times, a module within the 2000 Northern Ireland Life and Times survey, is, therefore, a milestone piece of research. It is particularly welcome because it not only asks men and boys about issues that affect themselves, but it also asks women and girls for their opinions on these subjects. This dimension makes the Men's Life and Times module unique.

The problem with men

It would appear that men and boys are rarely given much attention until they are seen as a problem. What we do know about them tends to come from either a 'deficit model' (their shortcomings) or a 'default model' (where the focus is on females, and so, by default, the rest of the people in the study are male). This obviously does little to increase our understanding. One thing is sure – we know more about men and boys from the outside (their actions and behaviours) than from the inside (their thoughts, feelings, attitudes and values).

The media, however, is increasingly filled with headlines such as 'Men Behaving Badly' or 'Crisis in Manhood'. They are always keen to highlight shocking statistics such as:

- Males born today in Northern Ireland can expect to live until they are 74.5 years old, while females can expect to live until they are 79.6 years old. However, in the most deprived wards (using the Noble Multiple Deprivation Measures) these figures drop to 71.4 and 77.1 years respectively (McWhirter, 2002).
- Girls consistently outperform boys by attaining the highest level of academic achievement in Northern Ireland. In 1999/2000, 43 per cent of girls left school with at least two A levels compared with 29 per cent of boys. During this period, over twice as many boys as girls left school with no GCSEs (Bonner and Rea, 2002). After leaving secondary school, girls are also more likely to continue their education (71 per cent compared with 52 per cent of boys) (Northern Ireland Assembly Research and Library Service, 2001).
- Men are much less likely to attend a General Practitioner (GP) than women and, subsequently, are more likely to die from treatable illnesses. The *2000 Northern Ireland Annual Abstract of Statistics* (Northern Ireland Statistics and Research Agency, 2000) shows that 20 per cent of females had consulted with their GP at least once in the previous 14 days while only 12 per cent of males had.
- In Northern Ireland and the Republic of Ireland the age-standardised cancer mortality rates are almost 50 per cent higher for men than for women (Walsh, Comber and Gavin, 2001).
- Nine out of ten people convicted by the courts each year in Northern Ireland are male, and 98 per cent of prison inmates are men (Northern Ireland Office, 2002).

- Slightly more than nine out of ten of those killed during the Troubles in Northern Ireland have been men (Fay, Morrissey and Smyth, 1999).
- During 2000–2001, 28 per cent of men drank more than the recommended sensible number of units of alcohol per week (21 units), or at dangerous levels (McWhirter, 2002).
- Between 1995 and 1999, male car drivers were responsible for 96 per cent of all alcohol-related fatal road accidents in Northern Ireland (Department of the Environment for Northern Ireland).
- Males in the United Kingdom are more likely than females to be the victims of a crime. Young men (aged 16 to 24 years) are the most likely group to be the victim of a violent crime (National Statistics, 2001).
- During 1999, there were almost six times more male than female deaths from suicide in Northern Ireland. These figures tended to be higher for particular groups such as gay men, young men and men in rural communities (Bonner and Rea, 2002).

These figures are only the tip of a very large iceberg. There are many other indicators that suggest that males are entering a period of turmoil and potential crisis. However, there is still little theoretical understanding of the issues facing local men upon which to base future interventions. Thus, there is a distinct possibility that men's needs will be sidelined until there is a major catastrophe, and that policy- and decision-makers will continue to react to emerging problems rather than formulating proactive, preventative strategies. One of the main obstacles to change is that men are perceived as only coming in two distinct varieties: heroes or villains, saints or sinners.

A threat to women's development?

Despite these warnings, men's issues are still rarely treated seriously in our society. On the one hand, there is a common perception that 'men's work' is only relevant to inadequate, 'needy' or gay men. On the other, men's issues may be viewed with suspicion as being a threat to women's development, and a mechanism to return to patriarchal social, political and economic systems. One thing is clear, however: there will be resource and policy implications if it is accepted that men have valid, quantifiable needs/issues, which require action. But there is an obvious danger here – it is likely that the government will find these resources by merely taking from Paula to pay Peter. Herein exists a real threat of potential conflict between the sexes, since the resources to support women's needs and work are, themselves, wholly inadequate.

Men's issues are women's issues

Nonetheless, there does appear to be a strong degree of support within local men's groups/work for a model that recognises that the future of men and women is both interdependent and complementary (The Male Link, 2000). This approach acknowledges that pendulum swings – which favour one group at the expense of the other – are detrimental in the long term to both parties, and that real equality requires trust, mutual respect and understanding. It also seeks to resolve issues by adopting the more inclusive concept of equality between 'people' or 'human beings' rather than the partisan groupings of men and women (Fowler, 2001). This approach seeks to move away from a divisive 'either/or' stance to finding solutions that accommodate and meet the needs of both sexes.

This viewpoint argues that though we should recognise and acknowledge the specific needs of each sex, it is futile to establish separatist projects that develop strands of men-only work which perpetually run parallel to women-only work. Men's issues (like women's issues) are everyone's issues. Everyone has a stake in the outcome: improving the quality of one group's lives will have a direct impact on everyone around them. Both groups have inalienable rights and needs, but eventually we must reach a position of convergence.

It is equally important to note that many (but not all) of the groups that exist to support males in Northern Ireland seem to reject the notion of creating a local 'men's movement' – complete with watertight ideological dogma, perceived adversaries and well-rehearsed slogans. Instead, they talk about 'men moving' – an evolving and responsive process of personal development and structural change, which recognises that this is not a battle of the sexes; that men can be their own worst enemy; and that the 'problem' with equality is that it is for everyone (Fowler, 2001).

The Cinderfella of resource priorities

There is a constantly growing set of indicators which illustrate that some men need increased support. Yet, at the same time, there is a common perception that men can/should look after themselves and have no distinct needs. Herein lies the Catch 22: society wants men who are more open to showing their weaknesses, sharing their emotions and who will ask for help. Simultaneously, those men who do are often categorised as 'whingers' and 'big girls' blouses'. Thus, male issues become hidden statistics, and males become the 'Cinderfellas' of resource priorities: unrecognised, ignored, often shoddily treated, with a strong case for redress of circumstances ... but never quite able to meet their Fairy Godmother/father who can recognise their potential, change their situation, send them to the ball and ensure a happy-ever-after ending.

YOU WILL GO TO THE BALL ... DEVELOPING INTEREST IN MEN'S ISSUES/WORK

Although work to support males is still underdeveloped and under-funded in Northern Ireland, the last few years have witnessed a growing interest in this field. There are currently a small number of visionary groups and individuals who wish to effect change and who are demonstrating, in practical ways, the positive benefits to the whole community of engaging with men and boys. This 'pulls' this area of work forward.

However, perhaps the most noticeable increase in interest has been the result of 'push' factors: the United Kingdom being forced into accepting European Union Directives, obligations arising from the Good Friday Agreement, the need to respond to crisis issues such as rising male suicide rates or young single parenthood and so on. These push factors – particularly new legislation and the introduction of a raft of public consultations and equality-proofing measures – have provided an effective impetus to raise the profile of men's issues:

- The Good Friday Agreement gave rise to the Northern Ireland Act 1998. Under this, two bodies (the Equality Commission for Northern Ireland and the Northern Ireland Human Rights Commission) were established to protect the rights and freedoms of all citizens. It is interesting that both these bodies have recently welcomed a discussion on men's issues and have reasserted that legislation should deal with the rights of both men and women (Dickson, 2001; Harbison, 2001).
- Section 75 of the Northern Ireland Act 1998 placed a statutory duty upon a range of public sector bodies to equality-proof their services, and makes explicit reference to 'men and women generally'. The upshot of this is that representatives of men's work have been in great demand to take part in Equality Impact Assessment Schemes, although they were rarely, if ever, consulted with before this obligation was introduced. This, in itself, is indicative of the sea change in the attitude of policy-makers and service deliverers.
- During the consultation on a Bill of Rights for Northern Ireland held in 2001, the Chief Commissioner of the Northern Ireland Human Rights Commission, Brice Dickson, publicly invited submissions that outlined the current situation for males.

• The Gender Equality Strategy consultation (organised by the Equality Unit within the Office of the First Minister and Deputy First Minister) has encouraged representatives of men's work to input to the process from the outset.

Simultaneously, there has been a swell of interest in local communities. Some of this has been driven by the vision and energy of enthusiastic individuals and groups; some has been fuelled by men's experience of discrimination and inequality; some has its roots in responses to legislative requirements or emerging crises; some has been developed by agencies looking to find a new niche in the service-delivery market.

However, while these developments are positive, they also bring certain dangers. Perhaps the most obvious of these is that future programmes may be developed by well-intentioned people based upon hearsay and stereotypes rather than upon knowledge and understanding.

REMEMBER TO BE HOME BY MIDNIGHT ... LIFE AND
TIMES SURVEY DATA THAT INFORMS DISCUSSION ON
NORTHERN IRISH MALES

Despite the fact that we are aware of all these things, there is still very little research into men's issues. This is why the Men's Life and Times module is so valuable. However, it is also possible to disaggregate the responses from all the other Life and Times survey modules (from 1998 to the present) by the gender of interviewee, and so it is possible to access a much more comprehensive overview of men's attitudes towards the total range of subjects covered in Life and Times surveys since 1998 (see Appendix III). However, this chapter will focus on three major social policy issues: work, family and health, and will only utilise data from the 2000 Men's Life and Times module.

Men at work

Despite many changes in the labour market at the end of the twentieth century (Department of Enterprise, Trade and Industry, 2002), there are still some occupations that are seen as being the sole domain of either males or females. In order to test their perceptions, respondents were presented with a range of jobs, and asked if they are appropriate for men only, for women only, or appropriate for both men and women.

Table 1.1 shows that both men and women exhibit broadly similar agreement on which jobs are appropriate for whom. However, the strength of agreement differs for some occupations. Midwifery is still seen as being a woman's job, although more women than men feel it is appropriate for

Table 1.1   Appropriateness of jobs (%)

	Male respondents			Female respondents		
	Men only	Women only	Both	Men only	Women only	Both
Childminder	–	56	43	<1	47	51
Firefighter	52	<1	47	39	1	59
Primary school teacher	1	9	89	1	5	94
Midwife	<1	75	25	<1	59	39
Soldier in front line action	67	<1	31	56	<1	42
Staying at home to look after the children	–	34	64	<1	25	74
Priest or minister	39	1	58	33	<1	65
Secretary	<1	33	66	<1	21	78

both sexes (39 per cent compared with 25 per cent). Being a soldier in front-line action is seen as being a man's job. However, women are more accepting of women being in combat than men are (42 per cent compared with 31 per cent). Nine out of ten men and women feel that being a primary school teacher is an appropriate job for both men and women.

It is interesting to see how these perceptions compare to reality. Firstly, in relation to women as front-line soldiers, the United Kingdom Ministry of Defence states that

> servicewomen currently represent around 8% of total Armed Forces strength. The Armed Forces continues to seek to expand career opportunities for women, consistent with the need to maintain combat effectiveness. 73% of posts in the Naval Service, 70% of posts in the Army and 96% of posts in the RAF are now open to women. Certain front line posts are still closed to women on grounds of combat effectiveness, but women serve in combat roles both at sea and in the air. The Army is conducting a study into the effects of gender upon combat effectiveness. (2002)

Secondly, midwifery has only recently been a career option for men. The 1952 Midwives Act prohibited men from training and practising as midwives, and legal barriers were only totally removed in 1983. Within the United Kingdom, there were 86,495 people registered as midwives with the Nursing and Midwifery Council on 31 March 2002 (Nursing and Midwifery Council, 2002). Of these, 178 were male (0.2 per cent). However, these figures are the number of people registered, but not necessarily working, as midwives. The Northern Ireland HPSS Workforce

Table 1.2   Primary school teachers in Northern Ireland, 2002

	Teachers	Vice principals	Principals	Total
Male	779 (11%)	195 (32%)	469 (54%)	1,443 (17%)
Female	6,117 (89%)	423 (68%)	403 (46%)	6,943 (83%)
Total	6,896	618	872	8,386

Source: Department of Education, 2002

Census, 2001 (Department of Health, Social Services and Public Safety, 2002) shows that out of 17,642 nurses, 8 per cent were male. There were 1,232 midwives, none of whom were male.

Thirdly, although teaching in a primary school is perceived as being appropriate for both men and women, the figures tell a different story. At 31 October 2002, there were 8,386 primary school teachers in Northern Ireland (Department of Education, 2002), 17 per cent of whom were male (Table 1.2). However, more than half of principals (54 per cent) and around one-third (32 per cent) of vice principals were male. Only one in ten (11 per cent) teachers (excluding vice principals and principals) were male. The under-representation of men among primary school teachers is likely to continue: the 20th Annual Employment survey (Sutherland, 2001) shows that in 1997, 16 per cent of newly qualified primary school teachers were male. This figure was 33 per cent for the secondary sector. Johnston, McKeown and McEwen (1998) suggest several factors for this pattern, including societal negativity about males working closely with young children, the relative low pay of teaching, a male preference for obtaining a subject-specific degree and peer-group pressure.

There is a general feeling among Life and Times survey respondents that although role reversal is desirable, it is easier for women than men. Over half of both male and female respondents (57 per cent and 62 per cent respectively) agree or strongly agree with the statement that 'it is easier for women to take on traditional male roles than the other way round' (see Table 1.3). When asked how much they agree or disagree with statements about boys and girls at school, there is strong support, especially among women, for schools to encourage girls to train for jobs that were traditionally men's jobs: 68 per cent of men and 79 per cent of women agree or strongly agree with this statement. There is also strong support for schools to encourage boys to train for jobs that were traditionally women's jobs: 68 per cent of men and 76 per cent of women agree or strongly agree with this statement.

The work–life balance debate is very topical, and there are a range of initiatives supporting this, such as the Northern Ireland Work–Life

Table 1.3   Role/occupation reversal (% agreeing or strongly agreeing)

	Men	Women
It is easier for women to take on traditional male roles than the other way round	57	62
Schools should encourage girls to train for jobs that were traditionally men's jobs	68	79
Schools should encourage boys to train for jobs that were traditionally women's jobs	68	76

Balance campaign, supported by the Department for Employment and Learning and Business in the Community. Among Life and Times survey respondents, 30 per cent of working men and 6 per cent of working women worked over 40 hours per week. However, are people working such long hours by choice? Three out of five men and women feel the opposite, and agree or strongly agree that 'most workplaces expect so much of their employees that men can't get enough time to spend with their families'. Paradoxically, similar proportions of both men and women agree or strongly agree that 'many fathers choose to work such long hours that it damages family life'. Cynics might suggest that while there is strong support in some quarters for the introduction of family-friendly policies, moves in this direction may have been accelerated by European Union Directives. Among Life and Times survey respondents, there is some support for the idea that 'most workplaces these days give unfair advantages to people with children' – 26 per cent of men and 29 per cent of women agree or strongly agree with this. Unexpectedly, this view is held by more people with children aged 16 years or under, than by people without children in this age group (32 per cent and 25 per cent respectively). However, the latter group are more likely to say that they did not know. For a fuller discussion of men and women's attitudes towards work and work patterns, see Chapter 5 in this volume.

Men in the family

As highlighted earlier, there have been numerous legislative changes in Northern Ireland, heavily influenced by the European Union, which have benefited parents, and men in particular. For example:

- The Maternity and Parental Leave Regulations (Northern Ireland) 1999 of the Employment Relations (Northern Ireland) Order 1999, recognised fathers' as well as mothers' need for increased time with their children during their formative years by introducing 13 weeks unpaid parental leave for each child up until the age of five years.

Table 1.4   Attitudes towards men and children (% agreeing or strongly agreeing)

	Men	Women
All men should have the right to some paid paternity leave	77	82
Clinics for expectant mothers should also provide practical advice to fathers on caring for a baby	80	89
Men can care for children just as well as women can	59	67

- The Employment Bill (Northern Ireland) 2002 established an increased range of family-friendly policies including the right to two weeks paid paternity leave (from April 2003). This mirrors the Employment Act 2002 in England, Scotland and Wales.

Results from the Life and Times survey show that these measures are in line with respondents' attitudes. There is strong support for the provision of some paid paternity leave. Over three-quarters of men and women (77 per cent and 82 per cent respectively) believe that 'all men should have the right to some paid paternity leave'. There is also very strong support, especially among women, that 'clinics for expectant mothers should also provide practical advice to fathers on caring for a baby': 80 per cent for men and 89 per cent for women. Perhaps surprisingly, fewer men (59 per cent) than women (67 per cent) agree or strongly agree that 'men can care for children just as well as women can' (see Table 1.4). Responses to this third statement in particular differ strongly by age group. Younger men – aged 18 to 44 years – show high levels of support for this statement, while men aged 45 years and over are less supportive. However, for women, support continues until age 54 years before falling.

Family law often raises contentious issues among both men and women. In recent years there have been calls for changes in the law to take more account of the rights of fathers, especially those who are unmarried. Recent legislative change includes the Family Law Act (Northern Ireland) 2002, which has increased the parental rights and responsibilities of unmarried fathers.

The feeling that mothers benefit from family law is identified with by nearly half (46 per cent) of male respondents to the Life and Times survey. This view is less popular among women: only one-third (34 per cent) agree in some way that 'family law upholds the rights of women more than men'. However, 14 per cent of men and 15 per cent of women say that they don't know.

However, when asked if after separation or divorce, the children should always stay with their mother, responses are broadly similar among both men and women. Just less than one in four respondents (23 per cent) agree with the statement. However, around one-third of respondents (33 per cent) say that they neither agree nor disagree. It is not possible to interpret their motives for this response – perhaps it reflects the idea that it depends on individual circumstances. Responses to this question are significant when analysed by age, gender and marital status. In particular, 41 per cent of women who are separated or divorced agree or strongly agree with this statement, compared with 17 per cent of separated or divorced men. There is also a correlation with age: 16 per cent of 18- to 24-year-olds agree with the statement, compared with 35 per cent of those aged 65 years and over. A majority of men (57 per cent) feel that 'earning money should be the priority for a man rather than bringing up children'. This view is supported by 48 per cent of women. There is a very strong age dimension to responses: while 47 per cent of men aged 18 to 24 years agree with the statement, the relevant figure for men aged 65 years and over is 78 per cent. For women, the figures for these age groups are 26 per cent and 75 per cent respectively.

Domestic abuse

Domestic abuse is a serious problem in our society, which affects all members of the family. In 2000, police in Northern Ireland attended 14,520 domestic disputes, 7,335 of which involved physical violence (Northern Ireland Regional Forum on Domestic Violence). As with all crime statistics, these figures only record reported incidences, and are unlikely to reflect the actual number of offences.

One common perception is that men are nearly always the perpetrators of abuse or violence in domestic situations. This is also reflected in the reporting of such crimes to the police. Yet, for men who are the perpetrators of domestic abuse and wish to do something to change their behaviour, there are few programmes that are outside the custodial system. Interestingly, among Life and Times survey respondents, there is support by 86 per cent of men and 90 per cent of women for such courses to be made widely available.

Simultaneously, more than two-thirds of respondents agree or strongly agree with the statement that 'violence by women against men happens more than people think'. This view is held by 71 per cent of men and 69 per cent of women. Only 8 per cent of men and 9 per cent of women disagree or strongly disagree with this.

Contraception

Male contraception has regularly hit the news in the last few years. For example, a drug used to treat Gaucher's disease may also work as a male contraceptive, and tapeworms could be the source of a new form of

Table 1.5   Attitudes towards male contraception (% agreeing or strongly agreeing)

	Men	Women
The male pill is a good idea*	48	53
Most men wouldn't take the pill even if it were available	44	58
Most women wouldn't trust men to take the pill anyway	67	73
Most women would prefer to be in control of their own contraception	72	78

* excludes respondents who say that contraception of any kind is wrong

contraception for both men and women (BBC News Online, 10 December 2002). However, how is male contraception viewed by the general public in Northern Ireland? Excluding those respondents who think that contraception of any kind is wrong, more than a half of women (53 per cent) and just under a half of men (48 per cent) think that 'the male pill is a good idea' (see Table 1.5).

However, respondents also appear to have many reservations about male contraception: 44 per cent of men and 58 per cent of women believe that 'most men wouldn't take the pill even if it were available'. More than two-thirds of respondents (67 per cent of men and 73 per cent of women) think that 'most women wouldn't trust men to take the pill anyway'. Additionally, 72 per cent of men and 78 per cent of women feel that 'most women would prefer to be in control of their own contraception'. These figures highlight an important discrepancy among attitudes: while there is general support for the idea of the male pill, there is simultaneously a strong feeling that women wouldn't want or trust men to use it. Does this leave men with a no-win situation?

Men and health

Men's health has received significant attention in recent years. For example, the Men's Health Forum in Ireland and similar United Kingdom and pan-European bodies aim to improve the health of men and men's health services through collaborative research and lobbying for policy change. Much academic research has also focused on the health differentials between men and women, for example, Annandale and Hunt (2000) and McDonough and Walters (2001). This has explored the perception that 'women are sicker and men die quicker'. Despite this attention, there is a feeling among more than one-third of Life and Times survey respondents that 'men's health is not taken seriously by the health services' (see Table 1.6).

Prevention is seen as an important strategy within health policy, and Well Woman Clinics – that is, special clinics just for women where they can get check-ups, advice or health information – are commonplace in many GP surgeries. Well Man Clinics have also been set up, although not

Table 1.6   Attitudes towards men's health (% agreeing or strongly agreeing)

	Men	Women
Men's health is not taken seriously by the health services	38	36
Men need less emotional support than women	30	20
Men should spend more time talking about their feelings	57	66
Men fear failure more than women	51	49

to the same extent. Among Life and Times survey respondents the perceived need for Well Man Clinics is very strong. It is interesting that support is especially strong among women – the provision of such clinics is supported by 84 per cent of men and 90 per cent of women.

However, having identified Well Man Clinics as a good idea, only 57 per cent of men and 50 per cent of women think that they would actually be used in practice. Men as then asked if they themselves would ever use this service if it was provided in their own doctor's surgery. Just under two-thirds (63 per cent) say that they would – more than the proportion of men who say that in general many men would use a Well Man Clinic. In addition, 2 per cent of men say that they have used this service in the past.

In terms of emotional health, nearly half of men (46 per cent) and more women (55 per cent) disagree with the statement that 'men need less emotional support than women do'. In addition, over half of men and two-thirds of women think that 'men should spend more time talking about their feelings' (Table 1.6). In particular, the age group of men showing least support for this statement is the youngest group (18- to 24-year-olds). This is a worrying finding, given the high rate of young male suicide (Bonner and Rea, 2002).

Respondents were also asked if they think that there is a need for a helpline run by men for men who need support and advice through difficult times like relationship breakdown, unemployment and bereavement. Just over half of both men and women (51 per cent and 53 per cent respectively) feel that there is a need for such a helpline. Only 22 per cent of men and 14 per cent of women definitely say no. A substantial minority (14 per cent of men and 22 per cent of women) say yes, but with the stipulation that there is also one for women. A smaller minority (5 per cent and 4 per cent of men and women respectively) say that it depends.

Although there is strong support for a helpline run for men and by men, respondents are sceptical about whether men would be more likely to use such a helpline. Again, men were asked if they would be more likely to use a helpline that was just for men, and just over one-quarter (28 per cent) say that they would. The largest group of responses is from those who say that it would make no difference (45 per cent). Eight per cent of men say that they would never use a service like this.

Continuing this theme, there is also support from three-fifths of men (60 per cent) and women (61 per cent) for counselling services just for men. An additional 14 per cent of men and 20 per cent of women show support as long as there is also such a service just for women.

Approximately half of both men and women perceive that 'men fear failure more than women' (Table 1.6). Only around one-quarter of both men and women perceive the opposite. This has a huge implication in terms of seeking support, attending counselling, trying new things and embracing change.

AND THEY ALL LIVED HAPPILY EVER AFTER? ... POLICY IMPLICATIONS OF LIFE AND TIMES SURVEY FINDINGS

As highlighted earlier, there is evidence that some men are struggling to adapt to the emerging demands of a rapidly changing world that undermines many of the certainties held by previous generations. This, in turn, spawns a new set of needs. Paradoxically, despite this period of flux, there is a lack of substantive, rigorous, quantitative research into men's issues in Northern Ireland. The Men's Life and Times module is, therefore, a welcome and significant milestone in this field. It is the first large-scale random sample survey of attitudes and values towards a range of men's issues to be carried out here.

Within the Men's Life and Times module, there is evidence that men and women actually think quite similarly. The results show that across a wide range of social issues, there is strong support for both policy change and the introduction of expanded services to meet men's needs. This correlates closely with the findings from an earlier scoping study conducted by The Male Link with male respondents (Brady, Devine, Ewart and Fowler, 2000).

It must be recognised that some legislative policy change has occurred since the Men's Life and Times module was in the field, for example, the Employment Bill (Northern Ireland) 2002. However, there are currently few programmes that specifically target men. Indeed, even when such programmes are initiated, they tend to be problem-led and to seek a quick fix rather than being spurred by a desire to be supportive and visionary. The work that is undertaken is, for the most part, pioneered by the voluntary and community sectors. Their experience is that funding to develop interventions is scarce. This, in fact, mirrors our own experience of trying to access money to underwrite the Men's Life and Times module. Every funder that was approached – even those who said that they actively support gender research – refused to consider our application. The most common response was: 'sorry, but men's issues are not one of our priorities'. Perhaps this is another reminder that men and boys have to be a problem before attention is paid to them. However, there is also potential for conflict – raising men's issues may lead to competition with women's issues for access to limited financial resources.

Males are not a homogenous group with identical needs – although they are often treated as such. This is a self-evident truth when we consider that they constitute just less than half of the population of Northern Ireland. This huge body of people is comprised of young and old, urban and rural, disabled and able bodied, gay, straight and bisexual, employed and out of work, from majority and minority cultures/groups, in positions of power and not, educated and undereducated, powerful and powerless. This diversity is rarely acknowledged. Instead, males are often clumped together and seen as a monolithic unit (Whitehead, 2002).

There is also evidence to suggest that local men are seriously at risk of becoming alienated and socially excluded (Brady, Devine, Ewart and Fowler, 2000). Many feel that every aspect of their manhood has been castigated; that society is anti-men; that they are only associated with violence, abusiveness and hostility; that they are struggling to cope with conflicting demands; that they are branded as winners even when they may be losers or the victim; that their expectations and behaviour are limited by society's norms; that they have no place (Fowler, 1999). There is an urgent need for action. The Men's Life and Times module provides empirical evidence which can act as the starting point for an informed debate on the issues affecting males.

There is still a long way to go before men's needs and issues are fully represented and reflected within the policy agenda. However, it will be detrimental to both men and women if policy- and decision-makers continue to react to emerging problems rather than formulating proactive, preventative strategies. It is still uncertain if Cinderfella will live happily ever after.

REFERENCES

Annandale, E. and Hunt, K. (eds) (2000) *Gender Inequalities in Health* (Buckingham: Open University Press).

BBC News Online (10 December 2002) ' "Side effect free" male pill' <http://news.bbc.co.uk/1/hi/health/2557953.stm>.

Bonner, K. and Rea, D. (2002) *Economic Outlook and Business Review, June 2002* (Belfast: First Trust Bank).

Brady, N., Devine, P., Ewart, S. and Fowler, C. (2000) *Men's Attitudes and Values Research* (Belfast: The Male Link).

Department of Education for Northern Ireland (2002) personal communication.

Department of Enterprise, Trade and Industry (2002) *Northern Ireland Labour Force Survey Historical Supplement Spring 1984–Winter 2001/02* (Belfast: National Statistics).

Department of the Environment for Northern Ireland, 'Shame Boys' campaign <http://shameboys.com/>.

Department of Health, Social Services and Public Safety (2002) *Northern Ireland HPSS Workforce Census, September 2001* (Belfast: Department of Health, Social Services and Public Safety) <http://www.dhsspsni.gov.uk/publications/2002/workforcecensus.html>.

Dickson, B. (2001) 'Protecting the human rights of males in Northern Ireland, keynote address to the All-Ireland Men's Seminar' in C. Fowler (ed.) *Men and Human Rights: Papers from the All-Ireland Men's Seminar, Belfast 5–7 October 2001* (Belfast: The Wee Filourey Man Press) <http://www.mensproject.org/issues/aims.html>.

Fay, M.-T., Morrissey, M. and Smyth, M. (1999) *Northern Ireland's Troubles: The Human Costs* (London: Pluto Press).

Fowler, C. (1999) *Report on the Initial Meeting of Individuals/Organisations Interested in Men's Issues and Work with Men, Grosvenor House, Belfast, Monday 15th March 1999* (Belfast: The Men's Project) <http://www.mensproject.org/issues/report.pdf>.

Fowler, C. (2001) *Response to 'Making a Bill of Rights for Northern Ireland'* (Belfast: The Men's Project).

Harbison, J. (2001) Keynote address given by Joan Harbison, Chief Commissioner, the Equality Commission for Northern Ireland, at the launch of Men's Life and Times module, Queen's University Belfast, 15 June 2001 <http://www.mensproject.org/jharb.pdf>.

Johnston, J., McKeown, E. and McEwen, A. (1998) *Primary Concerns: Gender Factors in Choosing Primary School Teaching* (Belfast: Equal Opportunities Commission for Northern Ireland).

The Male Link (2000) *Value Base* and *Aim* <www.mensproject.org/malelink.html>.

McDonough, P. and Walters, V. (2001) 'Gender and health: reassessing patterns and explanations', *Social Science and Medicine*, Vol. 52, Issue 4, pp. 547–59.

McWhirter, L. (2002) *Health and Social Care in Northern Ireland: A Statistical Profile, 2002 Edition* (Belfast: Department of Health, Social Services and Public Safety).

Ministry of Defence (MOD) (2002) *Equal Opportunities in the Armed Forces* <http://www.mod.uk/aboutus/factfiles/equalopportunities.htm>.

National Statistics (2001) *Social Focus on Men* <http://www.statistics.gov.uk/StatBase/Product.asp?vlnk = 7071>.

Northern Ireland Assembly Research and Library Service (2001) *Gender Differences in Educational Attainment in Northern Ireland – 2001 Examination Results*, Research Paper 05/01, August (Belfast: Northern Ireland Assembly Research and Library Service).

Northern Ireland Office (2002) *Report on Gender and the Criminal Justice System, Northern Ireland Office* (Belfast: National Statistics).

Northern Ireland Regional Forum on Domestic Violence <http://www.domesticviolenceforum.org/police_statistics.htm>.

Northern Ireland Statistics and Research Agency (2000) *Northern Ireland Annual Abstract of Statistics 2000* (Belfast: The Stationery Office).

Northern Ireland Statistics and Research Agency (2002) *Northern Ireland Census 2001 Population Report and Mid-Year Estimates* <http://www.nisra.gov.uk/Census/Census2001Output/PopulationReport/populationreport.html>.

Nursing and Midwifery Council (2002) *Statistical Analysis of the Register, 2001–2002* <http://www.nmc-uk.org/cms/content/Publications/Annual%20statistics,%202001–2002.doc>.

Sutherland, A.E. (2001) *Teachers Newly Qualified in 1997: Report on the 20th Annual Employment Survey* (Belfast: Northern Ireland Centre for Educational Research, Queen's University Belfast) <http://www.deni.gov.uk/teachers/newlyqualified97.pdf>.

Walsh, P.M., Comber, H. and Gavin, A.T. (2001) *All-Ireland Cancer Statistics 1994–96: A Joint Report on Incidence and Mortality for the Island of Ireland* (Cork: National Cancer Registry (Ireland) and Belfast: Northern Ireland Cancer Registry) <http://www.qub.ac.uk/nicr/all_ireland.htm>.

Whitehead, S. M. (2002) *Men and Masculinities* (Cambridge: Polity Press).

2

Information, Participation and Trust in Health Care

Ann Marie Gray, Dorothy Whittington and Kate Thompson

The concept of user and public participation in health care has received increasing policy and academic attention since the 1990s and is now at the centre of National Health Service (NHS) policy. Partnership is promoted as contributing to the enhancement of individual and local care quality. In the United Kingdom, each of the documents setting out the proposed reforms of the NHS (Department of Health (DOH), 1997; The Scottish Office, 1997; NHS Wales, 1998; Department of Health and Social Services (DHSS) Northern Ireland, 1998) indicated that services would be shaped through locality-based needs assessment and user consultation. More specifically, the documents *Local Voices* (NHS Management Executive, 1992), *A First Class Service* (NHS Management Executive, 1998) and the *Patient Partnership Strategy* (NHS Management Executive, 1996) all set store on the views of people acting as a positive lever for change. More recently, *The NHS Plan* (Secretary of State for Health, 2000) promised more information to empower patients, more choice for patients and more say in policy-making. The hope is that this will also help the NHS to cope with increasing need and demand for health within a cash-limited system by encouraging the public to use services appropriately and contribute to their own health by adopting healthier lifestyles and acting on professional advice.

The provision of good quality information is seen as key to the successful and satisfying involvement of patients in their own decision-making, the creation of more responsible users of health-care resources and an important factor in achieving the involvement of citizens in health-care decisions. Coulter (2001) argues that insufficient information about their illness, prognosis and treatment options is central to people's dissatisfaction with health care. Ill health in Northern Ireland is well documented. On a number of important indicators the people of Northern Ireland are both sicker and less well served by health services than other regions of the

United Kingdom. Northern Ireland has one of the highest death rates from heart disease in the world, its cancer survival rates are among the worst in western Europe and there are serious inequalities in health with regard to social groups (Department of Health, Social Services and Public Safety (DHSSPS), 2002a). It also has the worst hospital waiting lists in Europe (DHSSPS, 2002b). Understanding the way people obtain and use health-related information, and a better understanding of their attitudes to involvement in health-care decision-making, may be helpful in overcoming this disadvantage.

HEALTH-RELATED INFORMATION

Alongside traditional professional sources, a range of health-related information is now directly available from print and broadcast media and via the Internet. Brown (2002) estimates that at least 10,000 Internet sites purport to offer health-related information. In the United Kingdom, the National Electronic Library for Health and NHS Direct are designed to allow patients access to information, support and referral to services without encountering the traditional gatekeepers such as General Practitioners (GPs) and Accident and Emergency Departments. There appears to be a growing belief that accessing health information through the Internet is becoming commonplace, although little has been published about the extent of its use over more conventional information systems. However, there is evidence that access to non-traditional sources of health information is more readily available to more affluent and better-educated population groups, thus exacerbating the relative disadvantage of other groups (Golding, 2000; Nettleton and Burrows, 2003). The proportion of households in the United Kingdom who can access the Internet from home is 45 per cent (National Statistics Online, 2003) although the percentage of adults who say they have ever used the Internet decreases steadily with age and ranges from 95 per cent of adults aged 16 to 24 years to 15 per cent for those aged 65 years and over. In Northern Ireland, the Office of the First Minister and Deputy First Minister (OFMDFM) (2002) reports a digital divide in respect of general Internet access in relation to age and socio-economic group. The Continuous Household survey (CHS) 2000–2001 showed that only 22 per cent of heads of household had computers and access to the Internet <http://www.csu. nisra.gov.uk/>. However, the Northern Ireland Statistics and Research Agency Omnibus survey, April 2002, shows the percentage of Northern Ireland citizens with access to the Internet at home as 41 per cent (OFMDFM, 2002). While this percentage increase is in line with that anticipated by the CHS, and indicates that use of the Internet is growing, the most recent figures still show that the majority of the population are not using the Internet and do not have access to it. It is also clear that socio-economic grouping has an impact on access, ranging from 61 per cent in the managerial and technical grouping to 36 per cent in the skilled manual group.

So, how does the Northern Irish public obtain health-related information, including through use of the Internet, and what are their views on involvement and participation in health care?

In 2001, the BUPA Foundation funded a module of questions in the Northern Ireland Life and Times survey covering a range of health issues. These included where people had sought/would seek information; knowledge of health-care structures and the organisation of health care, including knowledge of complaints procedures and consumer bodies; and public trust in health professionals. These questions were asked of 900 respondents.

SOURCES OF HEALTH-RELATED INFORMATION

Almost one-third (31 per cent) of respondents have spent time in the previous twelve months seeking out health-related information. As might be expected, older respondents and those with a long-term disability (or caring for someone with a long-term disability) are more likely to have done so. Respondents with better educational qualifications are also more likely to have looked for health-related information, although neither social class nor gender make a significant difference. Of those who said they had looked for health information, doctors and health professionals are by far the most popular source, with 87 per cent of respondents approaching them (Table 2.1).

Books and the Internet are the next most popular sources of information cited by 18 per cent of respondents in each case, while 15 per cent would

Table 2.1   Sources used by respondents seeking health-related information (% using each source)

A doctor or other health professional	87
Books	18
The Internet	18
Leaflets	15
A friend or relative who is a health professional	12
A pharmacist	11
Someone who practices alternative medicine	10
A support group	6
Another friend or relative	5
A telephone helpline	2
Other	2

Note: respondents could identify more than one source

use leaflets. This indicates that the use of traditional printed sources is still common among respondents, despite the availability of new technology. Whereas Jones (2000) notes that family members and friends are very often the primary source of information, only 5 per cent of respondents in this survey say this was the case. Similar rankings were obtained when respondents who have not actually sought health-related information in the last twelve months were asked where they would go if they found they needed to. Doctors and health professionals are cited by 91 per cent, books by 10 per cent, leaflets by 9 per cent and the Internet by 8 per cent. Pharmacists are slightly more likely to be consulted by this group (14 per cent).

The figures for Internet use (18 per cent and 8 per cent) are substantially smaller than those found by the Datamonitor study (2002), which estimated that 32 per cent of Europeans and 43 per cent of Americans use the Internet for health information. In 2001, a major study showed that more Americans accessed Internet health information every day than visited their doctor or other health professional <http://www.pewinternet.org/reports>. While it is likely that the figure for Northern Ireland will increase in line with general Internet use, the Life and Times survey data also indicate that Internet use is strongly related to age and educational qualifications. Respondents who have used the Internet to find information are significantly more likely to be in a younger age group, better educated, in a non-manual occupation, and able to access the Internet at home. This is also the profile of those respondents who say they would seek information from the Internet. Interestingly, while there is no gender difference in the level of Internet use among Life and Times survey respondents, both the international Datamonitor study and the Pew study of United States Internet use suggest that women are more likely than men to use the Internet to seek health-related information. They also note that women are particularly likely to seek out information on behalf of another family member. In England, use of NHS Direct (by telephone or Internet) reflects exclusion of older and disadvantaged groups, and there is some evidence that women make more use of it than do men (O'Cathain, Munro, Nicholl, and Knowles, 2000; National Audit Office, 2002).

Life and Times survey respondents were asked to imagine that their GP had told them that they might have a serious illness but that further tests would be needed. They were then asked whether they would seek out further information or would rely on what they had heard from the doctor. Just over one-third (36 per cent) say that they would seek more information. Again these respondents are more likely to be young, better educated and in non-manual occupations, but in this case they are also more likely to be female. As Table 2.2 shows, in these circumstances, the most popular source of information is the Internet (38 per cent), closely

Table 2.2 Where respondents would seek additional information
on a hypothetical illness (% identifying each source)

The Internet	38
Books	34
A friend or relative who is a health professional	28
A doctor or other health professional	27
Leaflets	15
Another friend or relative	10
Someone who practices alternative medicine	10
A support group	8
A telephone helpline	7
A pharmacist	6
Other	1
Don't know	1

Note: respondents could identify more than one source

Table 2.3 Profile of respondents who would use the Internet as
an additional source of information (%)

Age	
18–34	50
35–64	47
65+	3
Highest educational qualification	
A level or above	63
Below A level	37
Gender	
Men	34
Women	66
Social class	
Non-manual	84
Manual	17
Access to Internet at address	78

followed by books (34 per cent) and well ahead of health professionals
(27 per cent). It may be, therefore, that Internet information is seen as
useful in backing up or validating the information that has come from
traditional sources, or possibly that referring to it helps patients to under-
stand and come to terms with what their doctors tell them. Table 2.3 shows
the profile of respondents who would use the Internet as a source of
additional information.

There is little or no evidence of real patients' use of Internet sources (as
opposed to specially devised tele-medicine packages) during or subsequent

to diagnosis. One qualitative study using well people as surrogate patients (Eysenbach and Kohler, 2002) noted that participants said they were using the Internet to 'verify what the physician said and look for alternatives' but that they would always go back to the physician to check out what they had discovered for themselves.

A number of concerns about these developments can be identified. Firstly, there is considerable debate about the usefulness, accuracy and reliability of information from an expanding array of non-traditional sources, and about patient and public capacity for distinguishing good from bad or about how people use the information they source. Panch (2002) found that, in practice, patients in a study he conducted did not feel that Internet health information had made much impact on their understanding of their health and their ability to make more informed decisions regarding their care.

Secondly, there is concern that far from controlling demand for health care, the wide availability of information may actually stimulate it. A major business analysis survey found that 21 per cent of Europeans who had looked for Internet health information asked their physician for a specific medication they had read about online <http://www.datamonitor.com>. NHS Direct, too, may have 'discovered unexpressed demand' (George, 2002) and patients will have differing needs for assistance with the interpretation of information they source and its application to their own situations.

Thirdly, there is substantial evidence that access to non-traditional sources of health information is more readily available to more affluent and better-educated population groups. Selwyn's (2002) study of technology, social exclusion and government policy-making shows that despite the United Kingdom's relatively high levels of Information and Communication Technology (ICT) use, coupled with the Labour government's drive to widen access, specific social groups are significantly less likely to have ready access to ICT. Rather than ICT being a weapon in the fight against social exclusion as envisaged by the Labour government, it could maintain and exacerbate existing inequalities. Golding (2000) and Nettleton and Burrows (2003) contend that, for the most part, ICT contributes to the reproduction of existing socio-structural forms of disadvantage. In addition, they stress that access remains so strongly socially patterned that those with the greatest need of welfare services are often the least likely to have access.

Finally, many professionals claim that the availability and proliferation of information and the availability of 'rival' information has combined with media interest in health-care scares and scandals to reduce public confidence in practitioners. Nettleton and Burrows (2003) point to O'Neill's (2002) view that the volume of information and contested claims can leave us confused and uncertain about theoretical risks, for example, the supposed evidence that certain drugs are risky, that fluoride in the water supply is harmful or that the training of doctors is inadequate.

PUBLIC TRUST IN HEALTH PROFESSIONALS

It might have been expected that the series of high-profile medical scandals in recent years, including the well-publicised evidence of failure of clinical performance, such as the retention of organs, the death of children after heart surgery at Bristol Royal Infirmary and the murder of patients by Harold Shipman, would have diminished public and patient faith in the medical profession. Pringle (2000) argues that the implications of the Shipman case highlighted a range of areas where patients' trust in GPs was misplaced and where systems and structures were shown to be deficient. It revealed the limitations of the regulation of the medical profession, the monitoring of the prescribing of controlled drugs, the monitoring of GP death rates and it shook the trust that patients have in doctors to put their interests first (Smith, 1998). Yet, on the whole, results from the Life and Times survey suggest that people place considerable trust in health professionals. The proportion of people identifying their doctor or another health professional as the best source of information and advice suggests that the Northern Irish public continues to place faith in the medical profession. Responses to a question about whom the public would rely on to provide information about a specific situation further illustrate this confidence.

Respondents were presented with the following question: 'if each of these people made a statement about Mad Cow Disease – BSE – who would you have most confidence in?' If the figures for hospital consultants and GPs are combined, a total of 41 per cent of respondents say they would have most confidence in a health professional (Table 2.4). Those aged 65 years and over have slightly more confidence than other age groups in their own GP, and have significantly less confidence than other

Table 2.4 Whom respondents would have most confidence in for information on Mad Cow Disease – BSE (%)

Scientists working for health research charities	31
A hospital consultant	21
Your own GP	20
A friend who is a health professional	7
A government official	5
None of these	5
Don't know	5
A journalist writing in a newspaper	4
A TV reporter	3

Table 2.5   People just can't trust doctors
as much as they used to (%)

Strongly agree	12
Agree	46
Neither agree nor disagree	13
Disagree	23
Strongly disagree	2
Don't know	4

groups in scientists working for health research charities. Across all groups, respondents have least confidence in journalists working for newspapers and in government officials.

On the other hand, when respondents were presented with the following statement: 'there have been so many medical scandals that people just can't trust doctors as much as they used to', over a half (58 per cent) strongly agree or agree with the statement and only 2 per cent strongly disagree (Table 2.5). The response to this question suggests that people do appear to be concerned with medical scandals.

Nevertheless, 71 per cent of respondents strongly agree or agree that newspapers and television programmes play up health scares just to get a good story. In addition, 89 per cent agree or strongly agree that doctors should be respected for the difficult job they do. In all, data emerging from this Life and Times survey suggest that public trust in doctors remains intact. Similar findings emerged from a MORI poll conducted in Britain in February 2002. Responses from 1,972 people showed that 91 per cent thought that doctors tell the truth and identified them as the most trusted of professions listed. Other public attitude surveys have continually pointed to a high degree of satisfaction with GP services (Gray, 1998), even when satisfaction with the NHS as a whole has decreased. Perhaps people are happiest with the services that are closest to them and that they most use, and it may be that they feel trust is an important element of the doctor–patient relationship. In her Reith Lectures, Onora O'Neill argued that trust should be guarded to the end, 'without trust we cannot stand' (O'Neill, 2002). Perhaps the public agrees. It could also be the case that their trust is very pragmatic. They may recognise a degree of sensationalism attached to the reporting of medical scandals and while they feel they can't trust the health-care system, they can trust their own doctors.

PUBLIC PARTICIPATION IN HEALTH CARE

Rudolph Klein (1989) has referred to users as the 'ghosts' in the NHS machinery and certainly for much of its existence patients have been viewed as passive consumers of services. Bradley, Sweeney and Waterfield (1999) remind us that England's first health strategy, *The Health of the Nation* (DOH, 1992), was formulated without systematic input from the citizens whose health was targeted. Yet, at the same time, there was increasing policy and academic attention being devoted to facilitating and enhancing public involvement. 'Working for Patients', the White Paper on the restructuring of the health service published in 1989, heralded the notion of the health-care 'consumer', a more pro-active user of services who could expect greater choice and accountability and more responsive services. *The Patients' Charter* was published by the Conservative government, under John Major, in 1991 in an effort to make the rights of service users more explicit (DOH, 1991). Subsequent analysis concluded that these reforms had a marginal effect on patient choice and did not result in the kinds of changes advocated by the architects of the 1989 review (Health Service Commissioner, 1994; Ham, 1997).

Throughout the 1980s and 1990s there was also a substantial increase in the self-organisation of people who had previously been constructed as clients of welfare services. These new 'user movements' developed considerably in the 1990s, although Barnes (1997) reported that power was still effectively located with professionals and bureaucracies. Although 'user involvement' had been the mantra of a range of health- and social-care reforms, especially the Community Care reforms implemented in 1993, the reality was that the task was greater than had been envisaged.

Greater and more accessible information is viewed by the Labour government as a key part of the strategy in relation to the goal of 'user empowerment' and the concept of user and public involvement is at the centre of health policy. *The NHS Plan* (Secretary of State for Health, 2000) pointed to the need for care to be shaped around the convenience and concerns of patients and argued that 'to bring this about, patients must have more say in their own treatment and more influence over the way the NHS works'. In Britain, the Plan has been followed by a flurry of activity including the development of a new independent statutory national body, the Commission for Patient and Public Involvement in Health, with Patient Advocacy and Liaison Services (PALS) in each NHS Trust. Patients' Forums have replaced Community Health Councils and a new Independent Complaints and Advocacy Service has been established. In 2003 a Citizens' Council was launched by the National Institute for Clinical Effectiveness (NICE). The purpose of this Council is to provide advice to NICE on topics relating to social, ethical or moral questions regarding the Institute's work. Membership of the Council is drawn from the general population and is intended to be representative of it. Coulter (2003) argues that this could provide a valuable source of evidence on how members of the public approach these issues. To date there has been less progress in Northern Ireland, although decisions about new health-care structures will include proposals to develop 'consumer representation' (DHSSPS, 2002c).

Attempts to involve patients and the public do raise a number of issues. Are patients and the public sufficiently informed for their participation to be meaningful? What evidence is there that public views and participation can genuinely influence policy-making? The assumption cannot be made that user and public views are the same, and so to what extent are 'public' views the views of an unrepresentative minority? These issues cannot be addressed in this chapter but the findings from the Life and Times survey help to inform us about the Northern Irish public's knowledge of the organisation of health care and the extent to which they wish to have a say in health policy.

The Life and Times survey included a number of questions about the organisation and workings of the NHS. The results in Table 2.6 indicate a low level of knowledge. While just over a half of respondents (53 per cent) have heard of the Patients' Charter, the proportion who know about their local Health and Social Services Councils, the watchdog bodies in Northern Ireland for health and personal social services, is dismally low at only 23 per cent. Thirty per cent of respondents do not know who they should contact if they wanted to make a serious complaint about their GP, while 26 per cent do not know who they would contact if they had concerns about having to wait at least 18 months for treatment.

Yet there is strong agreement that people should have a say in health-care decisions with 76 per cent of respondents believing that it is essential that if big changes to the health service were to be made, people living in the area should have a say (Table 2.7). A further 20 per cent say it is important. Opinion is divided on whether nowadays the government is better at involving the public in decisions about health-care planning, with 37 per cent of respondents agreeing or strongly agreeing that it is and 40 per cent disagreeing.

However, when respondents were presented with the following statement: 'nobody takes any notice of the views of local people when deciding to close hospitals', 78 per cent feel the views of local people are not taken into account (Table 2.8). This may be unsurprising given recent and ongoing

Table 2.6   Awareness of health-related organisations (% saying yes)

Have you ever heard of the Patients' Charter	53
Have you ever heard of your local Health and Social Services Council	23
Have you heard of the NHS Direct website	16

Table 2.7 Importance of public opinion in health-care decisions (%)

Essential	76
Important	20
Neither important nor unimportant	2
Not important	1
Not at all important	1
Don't know	2

Table 2.8 Local people's views are not taken into account with regard to hospital closures (%)

Strongly agree	28
Agree	50
Neither agree nor disagree	9
Disagree	8
Strongly disagree	1
Don't know	4

controversy about plans for acute health care in Northern Ireland. However, they are important findings at a time when decisions are being made about the future configuration of services and NHS structures.

The scepticism about whether or not public opinion and involvement can influence policy and management decisions may well be justified. Although the process of consultation has become integral to the development of most social policies, there is considerable debate about the best mechanisms for consultation and the extent to which participation makes a difference. The more progressive view of user engagement goes beyond entitlement to a set of rights linked to the consumerist approach to health care, for example, the right to be seen in an Accident and Emergency Department within a specific time or the right to complain. The aim is empowerment as represented by an ability to affect outcomes (Cook, 2002). While there is relatively little research to date, a few studies point to participation resulting in only limited influence (Barnes, Harrison, Mort and Shardlow, 1999; Pickard, Marshall, Rogers, Sheaff, Sibbald, Campbell, Halliwell and Roland, 2002). There also needs to be a more critical examination of the degree of involvement desired by the public (Coulter and Elwyn, 2002). It may be that there are many who are not willing to take on greater responsibility in terms of participating in decisions about their own treatment or in broader decision-making processes. Coulter (2002) concludes that if shared decision-making is to be moved into the mainstream, the role of the patient has to be recast into one where they take on a more active role. This, she argues, requires encouragement, information, education and training.

CONCLUSION

The results of the 2001 Life and Times survey show conclusively that doctors and health professionals remain the most frequently used source of health-related information in Northern Ireland, despite the growth in ICT and the very high-profile discussion of medical scandals and clinical failures. Only 18 per cent of people seeking health information in Northern Ireland use the Internet to find it. This is substantially less than is reported in the United States or in a range of European countries and may be a function of Northern Ireland's relative lack of domestic access to the Internet. There is evidence to support concerns expressed in research in Britain about a growing digital divide. Life and Times survey results show that people who use the Internet for health-related information are more likely to be from younger age groups, to be better educated, to be in non-manual occupations and to have Internet access at home. This may have the result of exacerbating health inequalities as increasing emphasis is placed on developing a health-care 'consumer' empowered by ready access to quality information. Interestingly, the Internet is the most popular source of health-related information for people seeking a 'second opinion' or confirmation of something their doctor has told them.

Respondents express a desire to be involved in health-care decisions that affect them but responses are split on whether or not the government is better nowadays at involving the public. However, the majority of respondents believe that no account is taken of local views in relation to issues such as the closure of local hospitals. It will therefore be important to continue to assess public views on involvement and participation, and to monitor the impact of specific initiatives geared to advance the aim of patient and public participation in health care.

Although the autonomy and status of the medical profession has been challenged by government and by a more informed public, the survey results suggest that doctors are still held in high esteem. While there is less evidence that people gain health information on the Internet than seems to be generally assumed, it may be that the growth of medical information available on the Internet will further result in the dispersion of medical knowledge. In the future this may alter the doctor–patient relationship and challenge further the concept of medical dominance. As one commentator noted:

> for decades we understood the professions as a conventional nuclear family, with doctor-father, nurse-mother and patient-child. But our

hope for total wisdom and protection from father is forlorn, our wish for total comfort and protection from mother unachievable, and the patient has grown up. A new three way partnership should displace the vanishing family. (Salvage and Smith, 2000)

REFERENCES

Barnes, M. (1997) *Care, Communities and Citizens* (London: Longman).

Barnes, M., Harrison, S., Mort, M. and Shardlow, P. (1999) *Unequal Parties: User Groups and Community Care* (Bristol: Policy Press).

Bradley, N., Sweeney, K. and Waterfield, M. (1999) 'The health of the nation: how would citizens develop England's health strategy?' *British Journal of General Practice*, October, pp. 801–5.

Brown, P. (2002) 'WHO calls for a health domain name to help consumers', *British Medical Journal*, Vol. 324, 9 March, p. 566.

Cook, D. (2002) 'Consultation, for a change? Engaging users and communities in the policy process', *Social Policy and Administration*, Vol. 36, No. 5, pp. 517–31.

Coulter, A. (2001) 'Editorial', *Health Expectations*, Vol. 4, No. 1, p. 1.

Coulter, A. (2002) 'Whatever happened to shared decision-making?' *Health Expectations*, Vol. 5, No. 1, pp. 185–6.

Coulter, A. (2003) 'Editorial', *Health Expectations*, Vol. 6, No. 1, pp. 1–2.

Coulter, A. and Elwyn, G. (2002) 'What do patients want from high-quality general practice and how do we involve them in improvement?', *British Journal of General Practice*, October (Quality Supplement), S22–S25.

Datamonitor (2002) 'Who is looking for health information online? A segmentation analysis of the online consumer', *Brief No. BFHC0470*, 27 November <http://www.datamonitor.com>.

Department of Health (1991) *The Patients' Charter* (London: Department of Health).

Department of Health (1992) *The Health of the Nation* (London: Department of Health).

Department of Health (1997) *The New NHS: Modern and Dependable* (London: HMSO).

Department of Health and Social Services (DHSS) Northern Ireland (1998) *Fit for the Future: A Consultation Document on the Government Proposals for the Future of Health and Personal Social Services in Northern Ireland* (Belfast: DHSS).

Department of Health, Social Services and Public Safety (2002a) *Investing for Health* (Belfast: DHSSPS).

Department of Health, Social Services and Public Safety (2002b) *Hospital Statistics* (Belfast: DHSSPS).

Department of Health, Social Services and Public Safety (2002c) *Developing Better Services* (Belfast: DHSSPS).

Eysenbach, G. and Kohler, C. (2002) 'How do consumers search for and appraise health information on the world wide web? Qualitative study using focus groups, usability tests, and in-depth interviews', *British Medical Journal*, Vol. 324, pp. 573–7.

George, S. (2002) 'NHS Direct audited', *British Medical Journal*, Vol. 324, 9 March, pp. 558–9.

Golding, P. (2000) 'Forthcoming features: information and communication technologies and the sociology of the future', *Sociology*, Vol. 34, No. 1, pp. 165–84.

Gray, A.M. (1998) 'Attitudes to the health service in Northern Ireland', in G. Robinson, A.M. Gray, K. Thompson and D. Heenan (eds) *Social Attitudes in Northern Ireland: The Seventh Report* (Aldershot: Ashgate) pp. 75–89.

Ham, C. (1997) *Health Care Reform. Learning from International Experience* (Buckingham: Open University Press).

Health Service Commissioner (1994) *Annual Report 1993–1994* (London: HMSO).

Jones, R. (2000) 'Developments in consumer health informatics in the next decade', *Health Libraries Review*, Vol. 17, No. 1, pp. 26–31.

Klein, R. (1989) *The Politics of the National Health Service*, 2nd ed (London: Longman).

National Audit Office (2002) *NHS Direct in England* (London: The Stationery Office).

National Statistics Online (2003) *Expenditure and Food Survey* January–March <http://www.national-statistics.org.uk>.

Nettleton, S. and Burrows, R. (2003) 'E-scaped medicine? Information, reflexivity and health', *Critical Social Policy*, Vol. 23, No. 2, pp. 165–85.

NHS Management Executive (1992) *Local Voices* (Leeds: NHSME).

NHS Management Executive (1996) *Patient Partnership Strategy* (Leeds: NHSME).

NHS Management Executive (1998) *A First Class Service: Quality in the NHS* (Leeds: NHSME).

NHS Wales (1998) *Putting Patients First* (Cardiff: HMSO).

Northern Ireland Statistics and Research Agency, Continuous Household Survey (Northern Ireland) (2001) <http://www.csu.nisra.gov.uk/>.

O'Cathain, A., Munro, J., Nicholl, J. and Knowles, E. (2000) 'How helpful is NHS Direct? Postal survey of callers', *British Medical Journal*, Vol. 20, 15 April, pp. 1035–6.

Office of the First Minister and Deputy First Minister (2002) *Bridging the Digital Divide in Northern Ireland: A Consultation Document* (Belfast: OFMDFM).

O'Neill, O. (2002) 'Reith Lectures 2002: a question of trust. Lecture 1: "Spreading Suspicion"' <http://www.bbc.co.uk/radio4/reith2002/lecture1_text.shtml>.

Panch, T. (2002) 'Internet health information: a London perspective', *British Medical Journal*, Vol. 324, p. 555.

Pew Internet and American Life Project (2002) *The Online Health Revolution: How the Web Helps Americans Take Better Care of Themselves*, 27 November <http://www.pewinternet.org/reports>.

Pickard, S., Marshall, M., Rogers, A., Sheaff, R., Sibbald, B., Campbell, S., Halliwell, S. and Roland, D.M. (2002) 'User involvement in clinical governance', *Health Expectations*, Vol. 5, pp. 187–98.

Pringle, M. (2000) 'The Shipman Inquiry: implications for the public's trust in doctors', *British Journal of General Practice*, May, pp. 355–6.

Salvage, J. and Smith, R. (2000) 'Editorial', *British Medical Journal*, Vol. 320, pp. 1019–20.

The Scottish Office (1997) *Designed to Care: Renewing the NHS in Scotland* (Edinburgh: The Stationery Office).

Secretary of State for Health (2000) *The NHS Plan: A Plan for Investment, a Plan for Reform* (London: HMSO).

Selwyn, N. (2002) '"E-stablishing" an inclusive society? Technology, social exclusion and UK government policy making', *Journal of Social Policy*, Vol. 31, No. 1, pp. 1–20.

Smith, R. (1998) 'All changed, changed utterly', *British Medical Journal*, Vol. 316, pp. 1917–18.

Streets, P. (2002) *The Patient and Public Involvement Transitional Advisory Board* <http://www.doh.gov.uk/involvingpatients/tab.htm>.

3
Lifelong Learning

John Field

Modern educational policies place great emphasis on learning in adult life. Across western Europe, governments are exploring new measures designed to promote the continuous improvement of skills and capacities among the adult workforce. Such views have become increasingly widespread since the European Commission issued its White Papers on economic competitiveness (Commission of the European Communities (CEC), 1994) and education and training (CEC, 1995). The United Kingdom government's Green Paper on lifelong learning (Department for Education and Employment (DfEE), 1998) and the Irish government's White Paper on adult education (Department of Education and Science (DES), 2000) each took its own distinctive approach. However, they both shared the common European concern with lifelong learning as a means of promoting citizenship and social inclusion, while investing in human capital and building the capacity to compete successfully in the face of rapid economic globalisation. Shortly before devolution, the Northern Ireland Office published its own proposals for building 'a new culture of lifelong learning for all where people regard acquiring new skills or updating their existing ones as part of everyday life' (Department of Education for Northern Ireland (DENI)/Training and Employment Agency (TEA), 1999, p. 2).

It is not only among governments that adaptability, flexibility and the ability to continue learning are seen as ever more important factors in people's lives. There is a widespread belief that those who learn new skills and reflect on their past mistakes are much more likely to succeed in their careers, their relationships and their sense of self-worth. A whole industry of self-help aids has sprouted up to meet the demands of people who want to change themselves (Field, 2000). At a more theoretical level, leading contemporary social scientists like Ulrich Beck, Manuel Castells and Anthony Giddens see knowledge and reflexivity as all-pervasive hallmarks of modern society (Schemmann, 2002). Empirically, there appears to be some evidence that access to learning opportunities, as well as the capacity for continuing learning through adulthood, can help to reshape patterns of inequality and exclusion (Field, 2000). Therefore, the wider shift towards the promotion and adoption of lifelong learning as a key pol-icy goal brings both opportunities and risks for individuals, organisations and communities alike.

Systematic research on lifelong learning in Northern Ireland has tended to conclude that participation in organised adult learning tends to be at a somewhat lower rate than in the rest of the United Kingdom. A series of analyses of survey data during the 1990s repeatedly found that adults in Northern Ireland were considerably less likely to take part in learning than was the case elsewhere in the United Kingdom (Field, 1997, 1999). General levels of literacy and numeracy among adults in Northern Ireland were judged to be slightly lower than in Britain (Sweeney, Morgan and Donnelly, 1998). While one recent survey (Sargant and Aldridge, 2002) reported a sharp rise in participation in adult learning in Northern Ireland since the late 1990s, the sample size was small and it would be wrong to place too much weight on this isolated result alone. By way of contrast, data from the Labour Force survey for 2002 are more consistent with the earlier findings. The proportion of the workforce receiving any training in Northern Ireland is still lower than in the other United Kingdom regions, while 24 per cent of the Northern Ireland workforce has no qualifications compared with 16 per cent in the United Kingdom as a whole (McGinty and Williams, 2002). Overall, there has probably been little change in Northern Ireland's relative position, with participation in adult learning generally falling behind the general United Kingdom level.

This is particularly surprising given that, on average, levels of educa-tional attainment among young people in Northern Ireland are compara-tively high by United Kingdom standards, both in schools and at university. Most studies of participation in adult learning conclude that, all other things being equal, the level of people's attainment in school and college is usually a very good predictor of participation in adult learning (Cross, 1981; Gorard and Rees, 2002; Sargant and Aldridge, 2002). We might therefore expect participation in adult learning to be higher in Northern Ireland than elsewhere in the United Kingdom, rather than the reverse. This pattern is not just an intellectual puzzle, significant though it is for our understanding of learning in adult life. It also represents a considerable challenge to policy-makers, employers, education providers and the wider community.

In 2001, the Northern Ireland Life and Times survey measured attitudes towards lifelong learning in Northern Ireland. While the government has announced a range of new initiatives in recent years, which are designed to tackle major problems such as poor basic numeracy and literacy skills, these new policy measures are still in their infancy. Much has been done to widen access to educational opportunities. Yet because adult learners generally make their choices on a largely voluntary basis – rather than attending due to a statutory requirement – their attitudes, perceptions and motives are vital if participation in learning is to grow. The survey findings cannot provide answers to all of our questions about the nature and distribution of learning by adults in Northern Ireland, but they do give us evidence of people's attitudes towards learning. The chapter starts by exploring attitudes towards adult learning and its outcomes. It examines people's views on the influence of family and schooling on adult learning, followed by a consideration of the financial aspects of adult learning. The next section looks at whether people's attitudes towards adult learning are linked in any way to their participation in voluntary and community activity. The chapter concludes by drawing out some of the lessons of these findings for the wider understanding of adult learning, as well as identifying implications for the current attempts to promote a culture of lifelong learning for all.

ATTITUDES TOWARDS ADULT LEARNING

Most adult learners are volunteers. This is not to say that no one is pressured into participation. On the contrary, significant numbers of people undertake learning in adult life because they are required to, whether by their employer, as a condition of benefit, or to meet the demands of a regulatory framework (Field, 2000). Nevertheless, unlike school pupils or young college and university students, the majority of adult learners are there because they personally have made an active decision to learn something new. Therefore, because adult learning is a discretionary activity, issues of learner motivation and perception are crucial to any understanding of participation, as well as to any attempt to increase it.

Overall, the findings from the Life and Times survey suggest that people generally hold very positive views on adult learning: 86 per cent of respondents agree that 'learning in later life opens up a whole new world'; only 2 per cent disagree. Table 3.1 shows that differences between the genders are minimal, although there is some variation in attitude by age, with young people, ironically, expressing slightly less positive views than those from other age groups. Even among young people, though, an overwhelming majority agree that learning in later life opens up a whole new world. There are also variations by social class. Once more, there is broad agreement on the positive function of adult learning, though this time there is a marked tail-off in support among people from manual worker backgrounds. Attitudes are more positive among the best qualified, and

Table 3.1   Learning in later life opens up a whole new world (% agreeing)

All	86
Gender	
Males	85
Females	87
Age	
18–24	82
25–34	88
35–44	88
45–54	85
55–64	89
65+	84
Social class	
Professional	89
Managerial/technical	91
Skilled non-manual	88
Skilled manual	86
Partly skilled	82
Unskilled	78
Highest educational qualification	
Degree or higher	95
BTEC Higher/HND/HNC	94
A level/NVQ 3	91
BTEC National/OND/ONC	95
GCSE/NVQ 2	85
CSE (other than Grade 1)	83
None	83

lowest among the least well qualified, but still within the context of widespread overall levels of support. At this very general level, then, the survey results confirm that broad public attitudes towards adult learning are very positive indeed.

Of course, one might expect broad acceptance of the value of adult learning in a society like Northern Ireland, where the education system has long commanded a high degree of public support (Osborne, 1995). Motivation also plays a crucial role in adults' attitudes towards learning, as well as in determining the decisions they make about participation. One important factor in persuading people to learn is the belief that it makes a concrete difference to their lives. For some, the main reason for participating is largely instrumental: in other words, they see learning as worthwhile because it is a means by which they can achieve specific, concrete goals, and not as an intrinsically desirable experience for its own sake. The Life and Times survey asked respondents whether they saw learning in later life as 'only worth doing if it will lead to something useful like a job or a promotion'. This allows us to see whether people view learning as something valued primarily as an instrumental means to a primarily vocational end.

Based on this definition, only a minority – albeit quite a large one – take a largely instrumental view of adult learning: 36 per cent believe that taking a course is only worthwhile if it leads to something useful, like a job or promotion, with 51 per cent expressing disagreement. However, there are wide variations. Young people are the most likely to take an instrumental view: 46 per cent agree with this view of adult learning, as against only 31 per cent among those aged 35 to 44 years. Motivation is markedly more instrumental among men (44 per cent) than women (34 per cent). However, there are much sharper variations by level of highest educational qualification (people with no qualifications are twice as likely to take the instrumental view than graduates are) and social class (under 30 per cent of professionals and managerial/technical workers take this view, as against 41 per cent of skilled manual workers and almost a half of partly skilled and unskilled workers).

In understanding motivation, evaluating people's beliefs about the goals of learning is only part of the story. We also need to know whether they think learning will actually help them achieve this goal. For example, people may think learning is only valuable when it helps them get a job, but they may also believe that learning is an inefficient way of achieving this goal. The Life and Times survey therefore asked respondents whether they thought courses or training necessarily led to a better job or promotion. Most people (70 per cent) agree with the view that learning 'doesn't necessarily lead to a better job or promotion', with only a minority of 18 per cent taking the opposite view. Scepticism about the role of learning in achieving a better job or promotion is more common among men (76 per cent) than women (65 per cent). It is slightly more frequent among middle-aged than younger or older people; it is also higher among people of higher social class. Speculatively, these different findings may reflect the differing labour market experiences of different groups, with training and education playing a particularly important role in supporting job seeking among women and young people, as compared with other groups. The survey findings also show that, in general, people believe that most employers value experience above qualifications, with 47 per cent agreeing and 29 per cent disagreeing. Significantly, all age groups and genders respond in much the same way.

A slightly different way of looking at the question of motivation is to consider the way people are affected by changes in their environment. Lifelong learning is often presented as a response to external change. Technological change in particular is often seen as an important driver of

Table 3.2 It is impossible for people to keep up with new technology (% agreeing)

All	57
Gender	
Males	56
Females	58
Age	
18–24	42
25–34	51
35–44	56
45–54	58
55–64	63
65+	66
Social class	
Professional	58
Managerial/technical	50
Skilled non-manual	57
Skilled manual	60
Partly skilled	64
Unskilled	69
Highest educational qualification	
Degree or higher	41
BTEC Higher/HND/HNC	40
A level/NVQ 3	52
BTEC National/OND/ONC	43
GCSE/NVQ 2	56
CSE (other than Grade 1)	66
None	64

adult learning. As Table 3.2 shows, 57 per cent of respondents agree that it is impossible to 'keep up with all the new technology around at work these days', although a significant minority of 29 per cent disagree. Both genders are united on this. Unsurprisingly, there are sharp divergences by age group, with only 42 per cent of respondents aged 18 to 24 years agreeing, rising steadily with each age group up to 66 per cent among respondents aged 65 years and over. Graduates, as well as respondents with qualifications similar to BTEC, are among those least likely to agree with this proposition. Unskilled manual workers are particularly likely to agree (69 per cent). It is quite difficult to deduce what the implications of these findings are for participation, as it may be those who believe that it is hard to keep up with technological change who are least likely to resort to training.

As well as relatively instrumental outcomes, the Life and Times survey also explored some of the broader benefits of learning, by asking respondents whether lifelong learning 'makes people better citizens'. The findings suggest that civic outcomes are strongly associated with lifelong learning: 57 per cent of respondents agree that lifelong learning makes people better citizens. Slightly more men (60 per cent) than women (56 per cent) hold this view, and there is more support among older people, reaching a peak among those aged 65 years and over (65 per cent). There are slight variations by educational qualifications; graduates are most likely to believe that learning fosters citizenship, while those with no qualifications are least likely to take this view. Social class is associated with clear divisions: almost three-quarters of professionals (74 per cent) agree that learning makes people better citizens, against 50 per cent of the unskilled.

FAMILY AND SCHOOLING

People's attitudes to lifelong learning are generally very strongly influenced by their family circle and their school experiences. There is a broad consensus among researchers on the significance of school in shaping individuals' attitudes to learning in later life (Cross, 1981). In general, those who succeed at school and college are much more likely to take up learning in adult life than those who leave school with the fewest qualifications. Recent research also suggests that other family members can play a role in persuading people to learn in adult life. For example, in a study of learning careers in South Wales, Gorard and Rees (2002) have shown that the influence of family can span at least three generations.

Most Life and Times survey respondents (80 per cent) believe that their family would encourage them if they decided to take an evening class. Women (81 per cent) are a little more likely than men (78 per cent) to say that their family would encourage them. There is variation by age, reaching a peak among 18- to 24-year-olds (with 90 per cent saying that their families would encourage them) and declining to 67 per cent among those aged 65 years and over. This is largely predictable, given the general association in most people's minds between education and youth, and even this should be seen in the context of a clear majority among all age groups who say that their family would offer encouragement. Relatively few people expect their families to be discouraging; rather, those who do not expect encouragement think that their family would probably be neutral on the matter.

School experiences on the other hand are seen in a much more negative light. Less than a quarter (24 per cent) of respondents believe that school opened their mind and made them want to learn (Table 3.3). More women than men feel this, as do more young people and older people. Only among the 18 to 24 years age group does the proportion taking a

Table 3.3   School opened my mind and made me want to learn (% saying yes)

All	24
Gender	
Male	22
Female	26
Age	
18–24	32
25–34	21
35–44	23
45–54	23
55–65	23
65+	26
Social class	
Professional	40
Managerial/technical	28
Skilled non-manual	24
Skilled manual	21
Partly skilled	19
Unskilled	11
Highest educational qualification	
Degree or higher	44
BTEC Higher/HND/HNC	19
A level/NVQ 3	43
BTEC National/OND/ONC	28
GCSE/NVQ 2	19
CSE (other than Grade 1)	17
None	18

positive view rise above 30 per cent, but this falls sharply to 21 per cent among the next age group (aged 25 to 34 years). There are some differences by social class and educational qualifications. Respondents in the highest social class (40 per cent) are most likely to believe that school had made them want to learn while those in the lowest social class are least likely to hold this view (11 per cent). Similarly, many more respondents with a degree or higher educational qualification (44 per cent) than those with no formal qualifications (18 per cent) feel that school had made them want to learn. Overall, then, the majority of respondents appear to feel that their schooling did not deliver what is widely seen as a basic platform for lifelong learning: namely, an open mind and a desire to know more. This is surely a profoundly disturbing finding.

A more specific question on this issue led to broadly similar results. When presented with the statement that 'school taught me the skills and knowledge I really needed later in life', a clear majority of respondents

(70 per cent) disagree. Younger age groups are the most likely to disagree (76 per cent among the 18 to 24 years age group), while respondents aged 65 years and over are the least likely to disagree (62 per cent). There is a social class difference: 38 per cent of respondents in the professional and managerial classes believe that school did teach them the skills and knowledge they really needed later in life compared with only 12 per cent of those who were unskilled. Perhaps unsurprisingly, there is also a positive relationship between educational qualifications and views on the benefits of school. Respondents who had a degree or higher are most likely, and those without formal qualifications least likely, to agree that school had taught them the skills and knowledge they needed later in life (43 per cent and 24 per cent respectively).

On the other hand, only 13 per cent of respondents agree with the statement 'school didn't teach me how to think for myself', and the vast majority disagree. This strong consensus seems hard to reconcile with the responses to other questions about respondents' school experiences.

Selection at the age of eleven years is a key feature of Northern Ireland's school system. It has been suggested elsewhere, albeit somewhat speculatively, that this may also have an impact on learning in adult life, in that those who are able to attend a grammar school may then follow a narrow academic pathway, while those who see themselves as failures at the age of eleven may switch off learning entirely (Field, 1999). Results from the Life and Times survey certainly suggest that many people believe that the 11+ system means that most children feel that they are failures. Overall, there is broad agreement (55 per cent) with this proposition. Nevertheless, a significant minority of over one-quarter (27 per cent) do not take this view. Levels of agreement are lower among young people and older people, and reach a peak among the 35 to 44 years age group (62 per cent of whom agree).

PAYING FOR LEARNING

Any sizeable increase in lifelong learning would have serious financial consequences. However, while most people probably accept that initial education in school and college should largely be financed by taxpayers, responsibility for funding adult learning in any country is divided between employers, government and individuals. This partly reflects the extent to which the benefits of learning are shared among individuals, employers and the wider community. It also partly reflects the discretionary nature of adult learning. Yet because adult learning in the United Kingdom is largely non-statutory, local and national government funding for it is at best patchy. For many employers, too, spending on continuing training is treated as a discretionary cost, which should be controlled. The question of who should pay for learning in adult life is therefore of considerable general importance.

There is strong agreement among Life and Times survey respondents that workers themselves need to take responsibility for learning new skills: 82 per cent agree that 'if the Northern Ireland economy is to be successful, workers will have to take responsibility for learning the skills that keep them up to date'. There is also very strong support for increased government spending on lifelong learning. Almost three-quarters of respondents (73 per cent) agree that the government should be spending more on lifelong learning for everyone. Agreement is higher among younger respondents, and declines with age (although even among respondents aged 65 years and over, approximately two-thirds agree). Levels of agreement are also considerably higher among manual workers than among non-manual workers (80 per cent and 70 per cent respectively).

General support for higher public spending is mirrored by backing for financial assistance for specific categories of learner. As shown above, many people think that technological change poses a challenge. When asked who should pay the fees for a worker wanting to attend a two-day computer skills course that would help in their work, 70 per cent of respondents believe the employer should pay, 14 per cent that the government should pay, and only 8 per cent that the individual themselves should pay.

Views are more divided when it comes to paying for academic development. When asked who should support the studies of someone who left school without qualifications at 16 years, and wanted to take A levels or an access course, 60 per cent name the government while 28 per cent think the person should pay. Young people aged 18 to 24 years are less likely to believe responsibility should lie mainly with the individual (18 per cent) and are more likely to name the government (72 per cent). Respondents aged between 25 and 64 years are more likely to believe responsibility should lie with the person concerned. There is little difference in opinion by gender.

Respondents were then asked whether painting lessons for retired people interested in art should be free: 59 per cent think they should, while 32 per cent think that the person should pay for them. Men are more likely than women to think the person should pay, and women more likely to think the class should be free. Views differ by age with the middle age groups most likely to think art lessons should be free, while the younger and older age groups are more likely to believe that the person should pay.

When asked about their views on free training courses for four groups of unemployed people, a majority of respondents are in favour in all cases (Table 3.4). This ranges from 89 per cent support for free training for

Table 3.4   Free training and courses for unemployed groups (%)

	Lone mothers	*Ex-prisoners*	*People in their 50s*	*People in their 20s*
Strongly in favour	32	15	28	27
In favour	51	42	61	58
Neither in favour nor against	7	16	6	7
Against	4	13	4	5
Strongly against	1	10	–	2
Other	4	4	2	1

people in their 50s to 57 per cent in the case of ex-prisoners. Again, there are wide differences between the views of various sub-groups in the population. The lowest level of support is shown by respondents aged 25 to 34 years for ex-prisoners (51 per cent).

The Life and Times survey measured awareness of a particularly important government-funded learning scheme, the Individual Learning Account (ILA) system. ILAs were introduced across the United Kingdom in 1998, following the publication of *The Learning Age* (DfEE, 1998). They provided an incentive to participate in learning by meeting part of the costs. ILAs were suspended in 2001 as a result of allegations of fraud, and reintroduced in Scotland and Wales in 2003. Leaving the potential reintroduction of ILAs in Northern Ireland aside, the findings are still important for any future government-funded initiative of this nature. The fieldwork for the Life and Times survey was undertaken at a time when ILAs were in the news. The then Minister for Employment and Learning, Dr Sean Farren MLA, announced the suspension of the scheme in late October 2001, and this decision was widely covered in the media. Despite this media attention, only 23 per cent of respondents say that they have heard of ILAs (Table 3.5). Awareness of ILAs varies considerably between age groups, with roughly one-third of respondents aged 34 years and under claiming to have heard of ILAs, while nine out of ten people aged 65 years and over have not heard of them. Women are more likely to know about ILAs than men (27 per cent and 18 per cent respectively). There are striking variations by social class and level of highest educational qualification. Seven times as many respondents in the highest social class (43 per cent) as in the lowest social class (6 per cent) have heard of ILAs. Similarly, 52 per cent of respondents with degree level qualifications have heard of ILAs compared with only 9 per cent of those who have no formal qualifications. Among those respondents who have heard of ILAs, one in five have applied for an ILA card.

These findings provide considerable support for high levels of government financial support for adult learning. Although there is more backing

Table 3.5   Respondents who have heard of ILAs (%)

All	23
Gender	
Men	18
Women	27
Age	
18–24	32
25–34	32
35–44	30
45–54	25
55–65	15
65+	9
Social class	
Professional	43
Managerial/technical	31
Skilled non-manual	28
Skilled manual	15
Partly skilled	11
Unskilled	6
Highest educational qualification	
Degree or higher	52
BTEC Higher/HND/HNC	41
A level/NVQ 3	44
BTEC National/OND/ONC	31
GCSE/NVQ 2	27
CSE (other than Grade 1)	11
None	9

for some categories of learning and some types of learner than others, policy-makers could on this evidence expect the public to endorse higher spending in this area. It is ironic, then, that when government introduced a systematic programme of incentives in the shape of ILAs, public awareness of its existence is so low. As the survey was conducted at a time when ILAs were in the limelight, this suggests that publicity alone is not sufficient to draw a scheme of this nature to people's attention. It might even be deduced that public opinion might be more inclined to favour a series of targeted support schemes aimed at particular types of learner or learning, rather than a general programme of financial assistance.

SOCIAL CAPITAL

Since the late 1990s, researchers have paid considerable attention to the way in which people's learning is connected with other areas of everyday life. One body of research has been particularly concerned with whether people learn more when they are more engaged in their community and have more interpersonal connections with others (Field, 1999; Organisation for Economic Cooperation and Development (OECD), 2001). Because people are able to use these ties to cooperate for other purposes, they are often seen as an important resource. These ties are sometimes said to constitute social capital, a concept over which there has been considerable debate in recent years (Field, 2003). This is also important for reasons of policy and practice: lifelong learning does not take place in a vacuum and, particularly for the most excluded, the role of other organisations can be considerable. One obvious question concerns the influence of social capital on the way that information, skills and ideas are passed on from person to person. At a policy level, the government partially recognised this in 1998, when it said that the Action Plan for Northern Ireland 'requires the commitment and partnership of all the stakeholders in the economy, business community and education and training providers' (DENI/TEA 1999, p. 14). Statements from the devolved Executive have also recognised the importance of the voluntary and community sectors in achieving an inclusive culture of lifelong learning for all (for example, Department for Employment and Learning (DEL), 2002).

The Life and Times survey included questions on Social Capital in 2000 and 2001, which explore respondents' relationships and social networks. In an analysis of the 2000 findings, Murtagh (2002) pointed to the dense network of voluntary bodies, community groups and leisure associations which people join in Northern Ireland, helping to form a rich web of ties between people. By analysing social capital and lifelong learning in 2001, the relationship between them can be explored.

The results appear to support the view that there is a relationship between social capital and lifelong learning. However, the nature of that relationship is a complex one. As shown in Table 3.1, 86 per cent of respondents agree or strongly agree that learning in later life opens up a whole new world. Table 3.6 shows that respondents who say that a particular activity is important in their own leisure time are far more likely to

Table 3.6 Learning in later life opens up a whole new world, by importance of participation in various activities (% agreeing)

	Activity important	Neither important nor unimportant	Activity not important
Watching or taking part in sport	91	75	84
Community activities	94	77	84
Cultural events	94	77	84
Church activities	90	68	87

embrace a positive view of learning. In each case, the proportion of people who take a positive view of learning is well above the figure of 86 per cent for all respondents. So far, then, the findings would indicate that social capital and lifelong learning are positively related. Yet the findings also show that people who think a particular activity is unimportant take more or less the same view of learning as the wider population. It is among those who have no strong view one way or another that the proportion who view learning positively starts to fall. This is particularly the case among those who feel that church activities are neither important nor unimportant in their leisure time. This relationship is more complex when it comes to the analysis of respondents' actual activity levels in different types of groups and associations (Table 3.7). Those whose attitudes to learning are notably more positive include:

- Those who belong to a trade union or professional association, whether active or not.
- Those who belong to and have taken part in a church, a sports/hobby group or a charitable body.
- Those who belong to, but do not take part in, groups in the 'other' category.

In general, the results are consistent with the view that 'joiners' – that is, the active members of voluntary organisations – tend to be more positive in their views of lifelong learning than non-joiners. In addition, respondents who do not belong to a particular type of group hold less positive views on lifelong learning. Given government policy on encouraging local area partnerships as a means of engaging the excluded, it is worth noting that there is no particularly positive association between membership of neighbourhood groups and attitudes towards lifelong learning.

Table 3.7 Learning in later life opens up a whole new world, by level of participation in groups and associations (% agreeing)

	Have taken part	*Belong but have never taken part*	*Do not belong*
Political party or club or association	80	85	86
Trade union or professional association	90	92	84
Church or other religious organisation	88	83	84
Sports group, hobby or leisure club	89	85	84
Charitable organisation or group	89	82	85
Neighbourhood association or group	86	83	85
Other association or group	80	94	86

A breakdown of the responses of joiners to other questions suggests that different types of organisation are associated with different outlooks on learning. Table 3.8 presents the responses to three questions, which can be seen as broad expressions of particular value orientations. Three clusters of opinion can be identified.

Active members of political parties in Northern Ireland are more likely to hold an instrumental view of learning than average and – perhaps ironically – are less likely to see learning as associated with civic engagement; they are as likely as the rest of the population to take a resigned view of the difficulties created by new technology.

Active members of church groups, sports/hobby groups and neighbourhood groups are slightly less likely to adopt instrumental views of learning, slightly more inclined towards a belief in civic outcomes (although neighbourhood groups are a notable exception to this), and are slightly less resigned to the impossibility of keeping up with new technology (with church members constituting an exception).

Active members of trade unions, charitable groups and 'other' bodies are much less likely to take an instrumental view of learning, and are generally less resigned in the face of technological change. With the

Table 3.8 Attitudes to lifelong learning among respondents active in groups and associations (%)

	Instrumentalism: 'Learning in later life is only worth doing if it will lead to something useful like a job or a promotion'	*Civic engagement:* 'Continuing to learn throughout life makes people better citizens'	*Resignation:* 'It is impossible for people to keep up with all the new technology around at work these days'
All	36	57	57
Political party/club/ association	39	49	58
Church/religious organisation	32	61	58
Sports group/hobby/ leisure club	30	56	51
Neighbourhood association	33	51	53
Trade union/ professional association	22	63	48
Charitable organisation	23	57	53
Other association	23	49	45

exception of those involved in charities, they are also more inclined to associate learning with civic outcomes. These results confirm the complex relationship between social capital and lifelong learning. While joining a group or association makes a difference to attitudes to learning, what is more important is the type of organisation that is being joined, with members of some organisations being much more conservative than others in their approach to learning and change in later life.

The nature of this relationship remains largely unclear. Survey data of this kind cannot tell us very much about cause and effect. We know that social capital is connected with learning, but it is not clear in which direction the relationship lies, or whether both are themselves shaped by some other factor or combination of factors. This is, then, an area where considerably more research is required before we can be confident about the messages for policy and practice.

CONCLUSION

The findings from the Life and Times survey provide something of a mixed message about the prospects of creating a learning society in Northern Ireland. On the one hand, they suggest that people share an overwhelmingly positive view of the idea and practice of learning in adult life, and see their own family as likely to support them if they took up learning themselves. They are also able to perceive clear benefits from learning; these include very instrumental, specific advantages to the individual in terms of job and career prospects, as well as wider gains for society in terms of civic engagement and cultural development. Most people also recognise that while somebody else might pay the costs, workers themselves have responsibilities in respect of skills updating.

Yet respondents are far from being convinced that their schooling provided them with an adequate preparation for learning in adult life. Of course, the respondents were adults, who were therefore educated in the past, and who now live with the strengths and weaknesses of the education system in years gone by, rather than as it is today. Nevertheless, this finding is certainly consistent with the view that the Northern Ireland schools system is better placed in respect of formal, largely academic examinations success than it is in respect of preparation for continuous independent learning in adult life.

The findings on the funding of learning should also give cause for thought. There is strong support for increased government spending, as well as for free training for specific groups of learners. Most people also believe that the costs of training for technological change should be met primarily by employers. This raises the question of whether a learning society can really be achieved without significant growth in individuals' own spending. While the findings might be interpreted as suggesting a laudably high level of concern for community and social support, they might also be seen as evidence of a dependency culture that is incompatible with the individual independence and autonomy needed to cope with the new, fast-moving and unpredictable economic and social world. Such a world presents people with an environment that demands increasing flexibility and adaptability.

So far as the evidence on social capital is concerned, it seems that there is a correlation between joining groups and associations, and a positive view of learning. However, it is noticeable that more general attitudes towards learning tend to vary greatly depending on the type of civic engagement involved. In particular, those who are active in churches and neighbourhood-based groups tend to be considerably more conservative in this respect than those who are involved in other types of association. Given the strength of community groups and churches in Northern Ireland, this might constitute something of a challenge for policy-makers and providers alike.

Finally, it should be noted that in general there is a broad measure of agreement within the population on the value of lifelong learning. Some variation can be observed by age and gender. However, differences are most marked in respect of social class and level of educational qualification. This suggests that there is a considerable degree of consensus on most aspects of lifelong learning, and that a solid body of opinion exists which would favour higher levels of support from government and employers for people who learn in adult life. Government will need to target its efforts carefully if it is to avoid further marginalising the least well qualified and least skilled.

REFERENCES

Commission of the European Communities (CEC) (1994) *Growth, Competitiveness, Employment* (Luxembourg: Office for Official Publications).

Commission of the European Communities (CEC) (1995) *Teaching and Learning: Towards the Learning Society* (Luxembourg: Office for Official Publications).

Cross, K.P. (1981) *Adults as Learners* (San Francisco: Jossey Bass).

Department for Education and Employment (DfEE) (1998) *The Learning Age: Towards a New Renaissance for Britain* (London: The Stationery Office).

Department of Education for Northern Ireland (DENI)/Training and Employment Agency (TEA) (1999) *Lifelong Learning: A New Learning Culture for All* (Belfast: DENI/TEA).

Department of Education and Science (DES) (2000) *Learning for Life: White Paper on Adult Education* (Dublin: Oifig an tSoláthair).

Department for Employment and Learning (DEL) (2002) *Essential Skills for Living. Equipped for the Future: Building for Tomorrow* (Belfast: DEL).

Field. J. (1997) 'Northern Ireland – perspectives' in N. Sargant (ed.) *The Learning Divide* (Leicester: National Institute of Adult Continuing Education) pp. 91–8.

Field, J. (1999) 'Schooling, networks and the labour market: explaining participation in lifelong learning in Northern Ireland' *British Journal of Educational Research*, Vol. 24, No. 4, pp. 501–15.

Field, J. (2000) *Lifelong Learning and the New Educational Order* (Stoke on Trent: Trentham).

Field, J. (2003) *Social Capital* (London: Routledge).

Gorard, S. and Rees, G. (2002) *Creating a Learning Society? Learning Careers and Policies for Lifelong Learning* (Bristol: Policy Press).

McGinty, J. and Williams, T. (2002) *Regional Trends 37* (London: Office for National Statistics).

Murtagh, B. (2002) *Social Activity and Interaction in Northern Ireland*, Research Update 10 (Belfast: Northern Ireland Life and Times Survey).

Organisation for Economic Cooperation and Development (OECD) (2001) *The Well-being of Nations: The Role of Human and Social Capital* (Paris: OECD).

Osborne, R.D. (1995) 'Social attitudes in Northern Ireland: Education' in R. Breen, P. Devine and G. Robinson (eds), *Social Attitudes in Northern Ireland: The Fourth Report, 1994–1995* (Belfast: Appletree Press) pp. 32–48.

Sargant, N. and Aldridge, F. (2002) *Adult Learning and Social Division: A Persistent Pattern* (Leicester: National Institute of Adult Continuing Education).

Schemmann, M. (2002) 'Reflexive modernisation in adult education research' in A. Bron and M. Schemmann (eds) *Social Science Theories in Adult Education Research* (Munster: Lit Verlag) pp. 64–80.

Sweeney, K., Morgan, B. and Donnelly, D. (1998) *Adult Literacy in Northern Ireland* (Belfast: Northern Ireland Statistics and Research Agency).

4

Family Relations and Social Networks in Northern Ireland

Mary Daly

There is an extensive literature in the social sciences to suggest that being embedded within strong family and social networks serves many functions. Research indicates that having supportive social networks is closely correlated with the stability, healthiness and longevity of an individual. However, what has especially interested sociologists is the relationship between the nature of an individual's social relations and social solidarity and cohesion in society as a whole. Such relationships are especially pertinent to Northern Ireland given its history. In situations of political conflict and intercommunal strife, it might reasonably be expected that family would have a special significance. At the same time one might expect people in Northern Ireland to be cautious about which activities they participate in and to have a sense of distrust of political developments and the political process in general.

Against such a backdrop, this chapter focuses on a number of key aspects of social life in Northern Ireland, in particular, informal relations in the family and wider society. Using data from the 2001 Northern Ireland Life and Times survey, the chapter explores the frequency of respondents' contact with their family and close friends, their normative orientation towards relationships with family and friends, their sources of social support and extent of social isolation. Following this, there is an examination of aspects of the quality of respondents' relationships with the wider social and political spheres. For this purpose, levels of participation in key sets of activities, and attitudes to government and political actors more broadly, are explored. As well as investigating respondents' sense of empowerment or disempowerment, the analysis is framed in terms of social capital. It seeks to make links between respondents' personal or familial relationships and social capital. Comparisons are also made with attitudes towards family and social networks in Britain, using data from the 2001 British Social Attitudes survey.

FAMILY CONTACT IN NORTHERN IRELAND

The significance attached to family solidarity and how it is differentiated by genealogical distance go to the core of the social organisation of the family. One of the great sociological insights on the family is that, rather than being viewed as a fixed structure, the family should be understood as a set of relationships and identities that change over time. The family is a contested concept in the social sciences, however, and there is considerable debate about the nature of family ties in the context of changing patterns of social organisation. For example, Beck (1992) considers that modern society is defined by the impermanence of family ties. In contrast, however, McGlone, Park and Smith (1998) found kinship to be significant in the lives of most families in Britain in that the majority of people remained in frequent contact with their immediate family.

It is always difficult to judge the 'quality' of family relationships and family functioning from the outside. However, there are some indicators available: the frequency and form of interaction, people's opinions about the nature of family obligations and the extent to which they call on family members for assistance in times when they need support. Each of these, as well as the more general question of social isolation, will now be considered in turn.

CONTACT WITH CLOSE FAMILY

Table 4.1 shows how often respondents in Northern Ireland and Britain interact on both a face-to-face basis and by other means (such as telephone, letter, fax or e-mail) with particular members of their family. The following analysis excludes respondents who do not have the relative in question, or who reside with them.

There is considerable contact with close family members in Northern Ireland; 41 per cent of respondents see or visit a non-resident adult child every day and almost a quarter (23 per cent) see their mother on a similarly frequent basis. If other forms of contact are included, just over half (52 per cent) of respondents are in daily contact with the adult child to whom they are closest. Just over one-third (35 per cent) are in some form of contact with their mother. It is notable that few respondents report having no face-to-face contact with their close relatives. Of those relatives listed in the table, the least frequently seen or visited are siblings. However, nearly two-thirds (63 per cent) of respondents still see or visit the sister or brother with whom they are in most contact a minimum of once a week. It is interesting to observe that, in the context of a huge growth in other means of communication, such as telephone and e-mail,

Table 4.1 Frequency of social contact (%)

		Mother		Father		Adult child*		Closest adult sibling	
		Face-to-face	Other	Face-to-face	Other	Face-to-face	Other	Face-to-face	Other
Daily	NI	23	29	19	25	41	42	14	18
	GB	9	14	4	6	16	21	2	4
Several times a week	NI	31	34	28	26	24	29	23	26
	GB	20	31	15	20	22	31	12	16
At least once a week	NI	22	21	20	26	18	19	26	26
	GB	25	36	26	38	29	32	21	32
At least once a month	NI	13	6	17	12	9	4	18	14
	GB	17	10	18	17	18	11	18	22
Several times a year	NI	7	2	8	4	6	1	13	8
	GB	20	4	21	7	13	3	29	17
Less often	NI	2	2	4	3	3	2	8	4
	GB	8	3	12	5	3	2	18	7
Never	NI	2	6	5	5	–	3	–	5
	GB	2	3	4	8	–	1	–	2

Note: bases exclude those without the relative in question, those residing with this relative, and those not answering the question
* this refers to the adult child with whom respondents have most contact

face-to-face contact with close family members remains widespread in Northern Ireland.

There is some differentiation in the frequency of contact with particular family members. Parent–child contact is the most dominant. Over 80 per cent of people see or visit the non-resident adult child with whom they have most contact at least on a weekly basis, and for over six out of every ten respondents this contact is either daily or several times a week. There is a statistically significant gender difference: female respondents have more frequent contact with their adult children than male respondents. The next most frequent contact is with mothers. Three-quarters of respondents see or visit their mother at least once a week, and nearly a quarter see their mother daily. Physical proximity may help to explain this frequency of contact. Over two-thirds of respondents (70 per cent) live within a 30-minute journey time of their mother's house. In all, just under a half (45 per cent) live within a 15-minute journey of their mother's home and less than one-fifth (19 per cent) live more than an hour away. There is somewhat less contact with fathers. Two-thirds of respondents (67 per cent) see or visit their father at least once a week, with 19 per cent seeing him on a daily basis. Unfortunately, the available information on proximity is limited to how long it takes people to get to where their mother lives.

Although female respondents tend to have somewhat more frequent contact with both their parents (and especially their mothers) than men do, it would be wrong to imply that men in Northern Ireland are not in regular contact with their parents. Almost a half of men (45 per cent) see their mother either daily or a few times a week. There are no significant differences in the frequency of face-to-face contact with family by age or religious background. These patterns suggest that there are two tiers of nuclear family relationships: people have most contact with their adult children and mother, whereas contact with father and adult siblings is usually on a less frequent basis.

As seen in Table 4.1, the contrast between Northern Ireland and Britain is very striking. People in Northern Ireland are significantly more likely to be in frequent contact with members of their families as compared with those in Britain. For example, the proportion in daily contact with close relatives is approximately three times higher in Northern Ireland. Overall, it seems that contact among family members is a more regular and common feature of social life in Northern Ireland than it is in Britain.

CONTACT WITH THE WIDER FAMILY NETWORK

Contact with the wider family network shows a somewhat different pattern. As can be seen in Table 4.2, contact with secondary kin is quite frequent. When asked about contact within the previous four weeks, two-thirds of respondents have been in contact at least once with their parents-in-law, their brothers- or sisters-in-law and their nieces and nephews. The most frequent contact is with parents-in-law. Contact with uncles, aunts and cousins is less frequent – over a half of respondents have had no contact with these relatives in the previous four weeks. While these relatives are seen much less frequently than others mentioned above, it is important to bear in mind that between 10 and 20 per cent of people have been in contact with their aunts, uncles or cousins more than twice in the last four weeks. There is no statistically significant gender difference in contact with wider family members; the only exception is that women tend to have more frequent contact with nieces and nephews than men do. These results support the findings of earlier research, which suggested that the family network in Northern Ireland was seen as involving close relatives, as well as other relations such as aunts, uncles and cousins (Monteith and Pinkerton, 1996).

Table 4.2 also shows that the proportion of respondents in Britain who have had no contact with their wider family network is higher than for respondents in Northern Ireland. However, the proportion of respondents who were in contact more than twice in the previous four weeks is similar for both Northern Ireland and Britain.

In order to explore patterns of family contact, a range of indices were constructed on the frequency and form of contact with family members. Younger people are more likely to have frequent contact with family members, and respondents without partners report higher levels of contact with family members. Women are more likely than men to have more frequent contact with all relatives. This is in line with the literature, which tends to distinguish between female and male kinship. Women, and in particular wives, have been identified as devoting more attention to kinship relations than men (Allan, 1996). Women are said to play an intermediary

Table 4.2 Contact with wider family network (%)

	More than twice in last 4 weeks		Once or twice in last 4 weeks		Not at all in last 4 weeks	
	NI	*GB*	*NI*	*GB*	*NI*	*GB*
Uncles or aunts	18	12	30	22	52	65
Cousins	14	9	29	21	57	70
Parents-in-law	44	45	28	24	28	31
Brothers- or sisters-in-law	32	31	35	34	32	35
Nieces and nephews	32	28	34	28	34	44

Table 4.3   Opinions about family obligations (%)

	Agree		Neither agree nor disagree		Disagree		Can't choose	
	NI	GB	NI	GB	NI	GB	NI	GB
You should take care of yourself and your family first before helping other people	74	71	15	16	8	12	4	1
Adult children have a duty to look after their elderly parents	61	46	18	28	16	25	4	1

role in relation to contact between family members. Finch (1994) described them as the 'kin keepers'. So for example, it might be the female partner who contacts her partner's parents, or who takes on the responsibility for ensuring that there is regular contact between the different generations in the family.

NORMS ABOUT FAMILY OBLIGATIONS

Respondents were asked about their attitudes to a series of statements about family obligations. As Table 4.3 shows, respondents in Northern Ireland attribute high priority to family obligations. The view of 'family first' before other obligations is widely supported: three-quarters of respondents agree with the statement that 'you should take care of yourself and your family first before helping other people'. Views about the duties of adult children to look after their parents are also strongly held. The difference in the strength of opinion in Northern Ireland compared with Britain is striking. More than three-fifths of Northern Irish respondents (61 per cent) agree that 'adult children have a duty to look after their elderly parents', compared with less than a half of their counterparts in Britain (46 per cent).

PATTERNS OF SOCIAL SUPPORT

In order to substantiate the nature of relationships with family and friends, respondents' network of social support is examined. Respondents were given three different scenarios and asked to whom they would turn first if they needed help in each one.

Table 4.4 shows that the extent to which people in Northern Ireland and Britain confine their search for support to members of their immediate

Table 4.4   Sources of help in problem situations (%)

	Help while ill		Borrow a large sum of money		Feel down or depressed	
	NI	*GB*	*NI*	*GB*	*NI*	*GB*
Partner/spouse	56	68	20	24	45	54
Mother	14	11	8	12	9	5
Father	1	1	8	9	1	<1
Daughter	11	5	3	2	6	5
Son	3	3	3	2	1	1
Sibling	7	3	6	4	9	6
Close friend	3	4	2	1	15	21
Neighbour	2	2	<1	–	<1	<1
Other	2	3	38	37	11	5
No one	1	1	11	9	3	3

family is striking. For example, nine out of ten respondents would turn first to a member of their immediate family if they needed help with a household chore while they were ill. Just over a half (56 per cent) of respondents would ask their spouse or partner for help in this scenario. The next most popular source of help is mothers, rather than fathers, followed by daughters in preference to sons (although the gender gap here is considerably less than that between mothers and fathers).

There is some evidence that who respondents would turn to for help depends on the particular scenario. For example, close friends are seen as a potential source of emotional support for 15 per cent of respondents. However, only 2 per cent of respondents would consider a close friend as someone they could ask to borrow a large sum of money. Borrowing money is the scenario in which people are most likely to turn to formal sources of help (usually a bank or credit union). This is also the only one of the three scenarios where fathers and mothers are equally likely to be a source of help. The low presence or virtual absence of what might be thought of as more traditional sources of help is notable here. Neighbours hardly appear at all for example, either as the first or second ports of call. Similarly, there is effectively no recourse made to priests or clergy. Friends are called on only to a limited degree, and they are most likely to be turned to as the second, rather than the first, source of assistance. Judging from these data, friends in Northern Ireland are regarded primarily as a source of emotional support.

The comparisons with Britain are less marked than those found for contact with family. Where differences occur, there is greater reliance among British respondents on their partner or spouse and somewhat less reliance on mothers and daughters, as compared with their Northern Irish counterparts.

SOCIAL ISOLATION

In addition to exploring contact with family members, the Life and Times survey also asked respondents about frequency of contact with their best friend. The findings indicate that friendship networks are stronger in Northern Ireland than in Britain. As Table 4.5 shows, respondents in Northern Ireland see or visit their best friend very frequently and there appears to be no real difference in the frequency of contact with this person compared with close family members. More than 80 per cent of respondents (84 per cent) see or visit their best friend at least once a week, and over a half (51 per cent) see or visit their best friend more frequently. There is, surprisingly perhaps, no gender difference in this regard.

One in eight respondents (13 per cent) claim that they have no close friends. This group has no specific demographic characteristics that set them apart from other respondents. In contrast, the majority of respondents consider that they have between one and five friends in their workplace and/or locally. In terms of the identity of people's best friend (apart from their partner), approximately one-third of respondents name a relative. There is, therefore, some overlap between friendship and family networks. Neighbourhood or locality is generally more important than work as a source of friendships, although a sizeable proportion of people (50 per cent) would consider that they have between one and five friends among their colleagues. Considerably larger numbers of women than men have friends living locally.

Table 4.5 Contact with best friend (%)

	Face-to-face		Other forms of contact	
	NI	*GB*	*NI*	*GB*
Daily	21	9	21	11
Several times a week	30	22	31	25
At least once a week	33	29	28	34
At least once a month	11	19	9	16
Several times a year	5	17	3	8
Less often	1	4	2	4
Never	<1	<1	5	3

Based on these patterns of contact with family and friends, less than 1 per cent of Northern Irish respondents can be considered to be socially isolated, in that they have no contact with their family and say that they have no best friends.

SOCIAL PARTICIPATION, TRUST AND DEGREE OF EMPOWERMENT

Debates about the role of the family and of family ties are related to a broader interest in the general character of social participation and the fabric of social and political life. In a climate that is seen to be characterised by a general fracturing of social bonds, the quality of people's relationships within and outside the family is of increasing importance (Putnam, 2000). According to Allan:

> the segmentation of different activities, the separation of home from employment, and the changing position of family and the domestic sphere in people's consciousness have led to a major change in their patterns of social involvement and the significance of informal relationships in people's lives. (1996, p. 9)

There is a widespread theory that people's social participation has become more privatised. People nowadays seem more likely to engage in activities that are connected to their personal interests compared with the past, and they are less likely to be involved in locality-based activities. Participation in wider community activities is generally less valued (Beck, 1997). Civic participation in particular is seen to be declining, replaced by narrower forms of solidarity and social participation (Bellah, 1985). What might be called the density of social connections – the propensity of individuals to associate together, to engage in community affairs and to trust one another – is becoming fragile. At the root of this is a change in people's political and social values and behaviour.

PARTICIPATION IN VOLUNTARY GROUPS AND ASSOCIATIONS

Respondents were asked about their membership of a range of voluntary associations, some community based and some associated with recreational activities. These included a political party, a religious organisation, a sports group and a neighbourhood association.

Approximately a half of the Northern Irish respondents are not members of any kind of organised activity. At the other extreme, 8 per cent are involved in four or more of the activities listed. Men are members of a greater number of groups or associations than women. However, there are no gender differences for the relatively high membership of religion-related activities and the low level of membership of neighbourhood or local associations. There is a difference by religious grouping, with Protestants somewhat more likely to be members of voluntary organisations than Catholics. The main source of this difference lies in the membership of religious or church activities, which tends to be higher among the former.

People who are employed tend to be members of more groups than those without a job. A difference by social class is evident, with those in higher social strata being members of a greater number of organisations than people further down the social class hierarchy. In other words, the better-off sections of the population are more likely to be engaged in a greater diversity of activities. This general relationship between social class and social activity confirms the results of Murtagh (2002).

Table 4.6 shows wide variation in levels of participation by type of activity. For example, nearly a half of people are members of a church organisation compared with fewer than one in ten for a neighbourhood association or political party. Apart from religious organisations, the most popular forms of group membership in Northern Ireland are recreational associations and charitable organisations. While the questions tend to focus on the fact rather than the frequency of participation, Table 4.6 shows that once respondents are members of an association or group they tend to engage in at least a minimal level of participation in it. It is difficult to judge whether these levels of participation are, in an historical context, high or low because little prior information exists on this for Northern Ireland. However, the international literature shows great variation (Hall, 1999). Table 4.6 shows that, in comparison with Britain, Northern Ireland has a lower level of membership of associations or groups. This bodes ill

Table 4.6 Membership of, and participation in, voluntary organisations (%)

	Member		Have taken part in last year	
	NI	*GB*	*NI*	*GB*
Neighbourhood association or group	8	13	6	9
Political party	9	7	7	5
Trade union	17	24	9	7
Charitable organisation or group	24	19	19	16
Sports group, hobby or leisure club	36	44	33	42
Church group/organisation	49	28	41	22
Other association/group	12	18	11	16

for the development of a vibrant civil society in Northern Ireland. However, the extent of involvement in religious or church-related activities, as well as in those of a charitable nature, in Northern Ireland is especially remarkable in a broader United Kingdom context.

SOCIAL TRUST

Given Northern Ireland's history, one could reasonably hypothesise that trust would be a commodity or value in relatively short supply. According to Hall (1999), social trust is defined as the generalised willingness of people to trust their fellow citizens. In order to gauge the level of social trust in Northern Ireland, respondents were asked about their attitudes to a series of statements about how readily they can trust other people. It would not be an exaggeration to say that a high level of mistrust is evident. Table 4.7 shows that three-quarters of respondents (74 per cent) are of the opinion that 'there are only a few people I can trust completely'. However, such feelings of distrust appear to be less entrenched in Northern Ireland than they are in Britain.

The data suggest that respondents in both Northern Ireland and Britain approach each other with a high degree of caution. For example, approximately two-thirds of respondents feel that 'if you are not careful other people will take advantage of you'. People in the oldest age group (65 years and over) are most likely to express caution about trusting others but those in the youngest age group (18 to 34 years) are most cynical about whether 'you can be sure that other people want the best for you'. Over a half of respondents agree that 'most of the time you can be sure that other people want the best for you'.

If trust is, as Narayan (1999) characterises it, the propensity to cooperate, especially with strangers, the future of voluntary social relations in Northern Ireland and Britain looks relatively bleak.

Table 4.7 Feelings of social trust (%)

		Agree	Neither agree nor disagree	Disagree	Can't choose
There are only a few people	NI	74	8	14	4
I can trust completely	GB	81	7	11	1
If you are not careful other	NI	67	18	14	1
people will take advantage of you	GB	65	18	17	1
Most of the time you can be sure	NI	56	23	15	6
that other people want the best	GB	57	29	12	2
for you					

SENSE OF EMPOWERMENT AND DISEMPOWERMENT

A key aspect of political culture, and a marker of the general state of democracy, is the extent to which members of the general public feel that they can exert an influence on, or have a say in, government policy. Table 4.8 shows the extent to which people in Northern Ireland and Britain feel a sense of empowerment vis-à-vis government. There is a general sense of disempowerment: the majority of respondents in Northern Ireland (over 60 per cent) feel that people like them have little or no chance of influencing the government or of understanding what is going on. Furthermore, two-thirds of respondents (66 per cent) feel that the identity of the party in government does not matter very much since things go on much the same as ever. While people in Britain also voice a sense of disempowerment, this is less deeply embedded compared with Northern Ireland.

In Northern Ireland social class and religious background are significantly associated with feelings of relative powerlessness. Respondents in the two highest social classes feel more empowered than those elsewhere on the class spectrum. Catholics are somewhat more likely than Protestants to feel that they can influence government outcomes.

These three statements explore feelings of political efficacy – the confidence that people have in their ability to make effective demands and the ability of the political system to respond to them (Bromley, Curtice and Seyd, 2001). Judging from Life and Times survey findings, political efficacy would appear to be fragile in Northern Ireland. The history of Northern Ireland is such that the democratic system, and especially local democracy, was incompletely installed here. The stop–start character of

Table 4.8 Sense of empowerment/disempowerment (%)

		Agree	Neither agree nor disagree	Disagree	Can't choose
People like me have no say	NI	65	15	16	4
in what the government does	GB	66	11	23	1
Sometimes politics and government seem so complicated that a person like me cannot really understand what is going on*	NI	63	13	21	4
It doesn't really matter which party is in power, in the end	NI	66	11	17	6
things go on much the same	GB	63	8	29	–

* this question was not asked in Britain

the new political institutions arguably only increases the general public's sense of distance from power and politics.

Further analyses of Life and Times survey data explored potential linkages between values and practices in the private and public spheres. However, there was only a low correlation (0.119) between people's sense of social trust (considered in Table 4.7) and their level of trust in the political process (as in Table 4.8). Nor is there evidence of the positive relationship found by Johnston and Jowell (1999) in Britain between social trust and people's links to voluntary organisations. One strand of discussion about contemporary life is that the private realm of the family has become more detached from the public sphere of employment, politics and community. There is no evidence that this is the case in Northern Ireland, not least because those who are well embedded in their families are also likely to have higher levels of social participation. Close family relations may be associated with a general sense of distrust and disempowerment, however, in that they reflect (rather than cause) a withdrawal from the more public sphere.

CONCLUSION

Overall what these data first tell us is that family and kin relations are a very important part of the constitution of social life in Northern Ireland. Family ties, and especially those with members of respondents' nuclear or immediate family, are active at a day-to-day level. One could, on the basis of these data, argue that people in Northern Ireland are very family centred. This finds expression not just in terms of frequent contact but also in people's value systems and their behaviour when they need support and assistance. There is no evidence of what Commaille (2000) calls a process of defamilisation, wherein the status of the family as a dominant form of organisation for people's private lives is weakening. Quite the reverse. When the information on the frequency of contacts with family and involvement in voluntary activities is compared, the former comes across as being very dominant. While there is not the evidence to argue for a substitution effect, one could speculate that family relations are so active in Northern Ireland that they serve to undermine any need that people might feel for a broader range of social participation.

Turning to the second focus of the chapter – social and political engagement and trust – the evidence is that both are on the low side in Northern Ireland. Hence, if it is the case as Johnston and Jowell (1999) point out, that democracies rely on a balance between political efficacy (the confidence to influence politics) on the one hand and respect for political authority on the other, Northern Ireland has a long way to go.

The evidence suggests a more complex set of relations in Northern Ireland as compared with Britain.

The survey findings show some interesting aspects of the fabric of Northern Irish society. Firstly, if having close relations with, and a strong reliance on, one's family is traditional, then Northern Irish society is to be characterised as such. Secondly, a very strong picture of homogeneity emerges from these data. Apart from some robust but varying gender differences, the attitudes and patterns discussed in this chapter do not significantly differ by such factors as religious background or social class. When it comes to family and informal relations, as well as to the political process, respondents in Northern Ireland have similar attitudes.

The assistance provided by Paula Devine and Katrina Lloyd with the empirical analysis for this chapter is gratefully acknowledged. The research on which this chapter is based was funded by the Economic and Social Research Council (Grant No: R000223682).

REFERENCES

Allan, G. (1996) *Kinship and Friendship in Modern Britain* (Oxford: Oxford University Press).

Beck, U. (1992) *Risk Society: Towards a New Modernity* (London: Sage).

——(1997) *The Reinvention of Politics* (Cambridge: Polity Press).

Bellah, R.N. (1985) *Habits of the Heart: Individualism and Commitment in American Life* (Berkeley: University of California Press).

Bromley, B., Curtice, J. and Seyd, B. (2001) 'Political engagement, trust and constitutional reform' in A. Park et al. (eds) *British Social Attitudes: The 18th Report* (London: Sage) pp. 199–225.

Commaille, J. (2000) 'The role of the family in establishing the social and political link: the double defamilization' in H. Cavanna (ed.) *The New Citizenship of the Family: Comparative Perspectives* (Aldershot: Ashgate) pp. 202–15.

Finch, J. (1994) 'Do families support each other more or less than in the past?' in M. Drake (ed.) *Time, Family and Community* (Oxford: Blackwell) pp. 91–105.

Hall, P. (1999) 'Social capital in Britain', *British Journal of Politics*, Vol. 29, pp. 417–61.

Johnston, M. and Jowell, R. (1999) 'Social capital and the social fabric' in R. Jowell et al. (eds) *British Social Attitudes: The 16th Report* (Aldershot: Ashgate) pp. 179–200.

McGlone, F., Park, A. and Smith K. (1998) *Families and Kinship* (London: Family Policy Studies Centre).

Monteith, M. and Pinkerton, J. (1996) 'Family, friends and neighbours' in L. Dowds, P. Devine and R. Breen (eds) *Social Attitudes in Northern Ireland: The Sixth Report, 1996–1997* (Belfast: Appletree Press) pp. 87–101.

Murtagh, B. (2002) *Social Activity and Interaction in Northern Ireland*, Research Update 10 (Belfast: Northern Ireland Life and Times Survey).

Narayan, D. (1999) *Bonds and Bridges: Social Capital and Poverty* (Washington DC: World Bank).

Putnam, R. (2000) *Bowling Alone: The Collapse and Revival of American Community* (New York: Simon and Schuster).

5

The Changing World of Work

Boyd Black

A NEW ENVIRONMENT

There have been dramatic changes in the world of work in the United Kingdom since the 1970s. Then, collective institutions run by trade unions and employers were dominant and were supported by government. The number of collective disputes was at an all time high. Legislation in employment relations was still underdeveloped. Since then, collectivism has been in governmentally approved retreat. It has been forced back by a combination of increased competitive pressures resulting from the strengthening of the European Single Market and globalisation, and by restrictive governmental legislation. At the same time, legal developments have increased the number of statutory rights in employment available to individuals. The emphasis has shifted to a more individualised approach to employment and a concern with the link between human resource management and business performance (Boxall and Purcell, 2003).

Politically, there was a change from a Conservative to a Labour administration at Westminster in 1997, which was confirmed in the 2001 general election. The New Labour administration aimed to promote labour market flexibility based on minimum standards and security of employment for all employees, while avoiding excessive labour market regulation. The inherited context of the promotion of private enterprise and the encouragement of a competitive economic environment was to be maintained. Within this framework the government hoped to provide a new partnership between employers and employees for the modernisation of work (Brown, 2000). In Northern Ireland this would mean building on already existing partnership institutions such as the Labour Relations Agency (LRA) – which performs equivalent functions to the Advisory, Conciliation and Arbitration Service (ACAS) in Britain – and following the lead in private sector partnerships set by firms such as Tesco.

In 1999, a devolved government was established in Northern Ireland (it is suspended at the time of writing) with responsibility for legislating for, and the administration of, employment relations currently lying with the Department for Employment and Learning (DEL). Historically, government policy in Northern Ireland has been to keep employment relations law and practice fairly closely in line with that in Britain, and this approach was broadly maintained by the devolved administration.

The economic context has been uniquely benign since the late 1990s, with inflation averaging only 2 to 3 per cent (after rising to over 10 per cent in 1990), real wages rising fairly rapidly since 1981, and with unemployment falling steadily since 1993 to the levels of the early 1970s (National Statistics, 2001b). The first two factors have served to dampen trade union militancy and industrial action. However, the third factor, reflecting the welcome expansion of employment in recent years, is generating labour shortages in certain areas and may be contributing to a change in the employment relations climate at the present time. The Northern Ireland unemployment rate is very low by historical standards and at 5.6 per cent (National Statistics, Labour Force survey (LFS), Autumn 2002) is now comparable to the United Kingdom average of 5.2 per cent and below that for Scotland (6.1 per cent), London (6.7 per cent) and the north east of England (6.7 per cent). It is 2.1 percentage points lower than the European Union (EU15) average.

While there is some evidence that falling unemployment may be benefiting trade union organisation, there is as yet limited evidence that it has had an adverse impact on employment relations. The United Kingdom-wide fire service dispute, which began in November 2002, may be an indicator of rising dissatisfaction among public sector workers about their perceived relative pay position. Low unemployment may also be contributing to a climate of more assertive individualism in which individuals are concerned about enforcing their rights.

This chapter combines data from the 2000 Northern Ireland Life and Times survey Work Orientations module with data from a number of other sources, including other Life and Times surveys, to provide an overview of the world of work in Northern Ireland. Successive sections examine the structure of employment and skills; trade union density; attitudes to jobs and working time; working conditions and work motivation; employment management; industrial disputes; earnings; and employment legislation. The chapter concludes by highlighting the urgent need to develop a partnership approach within organisations to achieve the level of work commitment needed in the modern economy.

THE STRUCTURE OF EMPLOYMENT AND SKILLS

Data from the National Statistics Labour Force surveys suggest that employment has been relatively buoyant in recent years, with the number of employees in employment growing by 10.9 per cent between 1995 and 2000, compared with a comparable figure of 9.7 per cent in Britain. Even so, the working age employment rate in summer 2001 was 68.5 per cent in Northern Ireland, which is lower than the United Kingdom average of 74.6 per cent. The Northern Irish figure is comparable with those for Wales and the north east of England, but well below the figure of 80.4 per cent for the south east of England. The female employment rate in Northern Ireland (61.4 per cent) is the lowest of all United Kingdom regions and is well below the United Kingdom average of 69.4 per cent. However, females make up almost the same percentage of the workforce (43.5 per cent in 2000) as they do in the United Kingdom as a whole (44.8 per cent).

Structural change has continued apace, with employment expanding in the service sector and contracting in manufacturing and agriculture. The industrial composition of employment differs from that of the United Kingdom as a whole. In Northern Ireland, 35 per cent of employees were in public administration, education and health in 2000, compared with the United Kingdom average of 25 per cent. These are areas of employment where trade union organisation and collective bargaining remain well established and where employment relations expertise is generally available in-house.

In Northern Ireland, only 10 per cent of employees were in banking, finance and insurance compared with the United Kingdom figure of 18 per cent. However, private sector employment in general, particularly in services such as distribution, where unions tend to be relatively weak, has been expanding relative to that in the public sector in the 1990s. However, this relative expansion is not forecast to continue into the next decade (Northern Ireland Economic Research Centre (NIERC), 2001).

Increased employment in private services has been accompanied by a continuing shift into smaller workplaces, as measured by numbers employed. While the majority of employees in Northern Ireland (52 per cent) work in establishments employing more than 250 employees, in the private sector this is only true of 31 per cent of employees; 85 per cent of businesses have fewer than ten employees, and 20 per cent of private sector employees work in businesses employing fewer than ten people. Employment practices, whether it is the prevalence of joint regulation with trade unions or the use of best practice human resource management, are likely to vary with the size of the establishment. The Department of Trade and Industry (DTI) (2001) found that 51 per cent of industrial tribunal applications for all jurisdictions in Britain came from workplaces with fewer than 25 employees.

Part-time employment in Northern Ireland, which makes up 21 per cent of the total, is less prevalent than in the United Kingdom as a whole, where 25 per cent of employees are part time (National Statistics, LFS, Autumn 2002). Many part-time workers are female, working in non-union employment in the private sector, an area of employment where many of the new statutory rights are very relevant. Temporary work accounts for 6 per cent of employment in Northern Ireland, in line with the United Kingdom average, reflecting the growth in fixed-term contracts in sectors such as education.

Another feature of the changing structure of employment has been the continued trend towards internationalisation of ownership and management, which has introduced new approaches to employment relations and is usually associated with greater professionalism in the human resource management area. The continued advance of new technology has also impacted on the world of work, resulting in the restructuring of traditional occupations and a demand for new skills. It is also reflected in the growth of employment in call centres and in the software industry, and has contributed to the flattening of organisational structures, with line managers increasingly taking more responsibility for employment matters.

The changing structure of employment is reflected in the changing occupational structure of the workforce, with a shift into managerial, professional and technical occupations. This is accompanied by a decline in the number of unskilled and semi-skilled blue-collar jobs (Gaffikin and Morrisey, 1990). The educational qualifications of the workforce reflect this changing occupational structure. Data from the 2001 Life and Times survey suggest that 25 per cent of those in employment in Northern Ireland have a degree or some form of higher educational qualification. At the same time, 29 per cent of those in employment have no qualifications at all. This is a particular problem among men and among Catholics, where the proportion with no qualifications is as high as 35 per cent (Table 5.1). It is noticeable from the table that, on average, women in employment in Northern Ireland are better qualified than men.

Table 5.1   Highest educational qualifications of working respondents (%)

	All	Men	Women	Catholics	Protestants	No religion
Degree or higher	18	18	19	20	16	24
Higher education, less than degree	7	7	6	5	8	6
A level or equivalent	10	8	12	9	11	9
GCSE O level or equivalent	27	25	28	23	31	25
CSE	6	6	6	4	6	9
No qualifications	29	35	23	35	24	23
Other answer	4	2	5	4	3	4

Source: Life and Times survey 2001

TRADE UNION DENSITY

Trade union membership in Northern Ireland has shown a small increase from 1996 to 2000, up from 235,000 in 1996 to 244,000 in December 2000 (Northern Ireland Certification Officer for Trade Unions and Employers' Associations). The latter membership figure is somewhat higher than total membership indicated by the LFS, which suggests that total trade union membership in Autumn 2000 was about 212,000 (though this figure is subject to a margin of error of + or −15,000). Trade union density in Northern Ireland, defined as the proportion of employees who are trade union members, has been above the United Kingdom average in recent decades. In 2001, 37 per cent of employees were members of a trade union in Northern Ireland, compared with a United Kingdom average of 27 per cent (National Statistics, LFS). This partly reflects the larger share of public sector employment in Northern Ireland, where density at 66 per cent is much higher than in the private sector, where density is only 23 per cent.

Density in Northern Ireland in Autumn 2001 was higher than in Britain for every category of employee: full time, part time, private sector, public sector, manufacturing, male and female. Northern Ireland has the highest regional density level at 37 per cent of employees, higher than Wales and the north east of England at 36 per cent. However, trade union density has until recently been falling quite rapidly in Northern Ireland, down from 45 per cent in 1992 and 41 per cent in 1996, to 34 per cent in 2000. Unions have not been maintaining their membership share of the growing numbers of employees in employment in the private sector, where fewer than one in four employees are currently trade union members. Density in small private sector firms with fewer than 25 employees is likely to average less than 10 per cent. Density appears to have recovered quite sharply in 2001, up to 37 per cent of employees according to the LFS, although this figure is subject to a 95 per cent confidence interval of + or −2 per cent.

The Employment Relations (Northern Ireland) Order 1999 provides a statutory procedure for trade union recognition. This legislation, together with the impact of greater European Union influence, may be shifting the balance of employer attitudes more towards approval of trade unions, particularly in larger organisations. But trade unions still face a difficult task in recruiting members in small private sector organisations.

Almost two-thirds (63 per cent) of respondents who took part in the 2000 Life and Times survey either disagree or strongly disagree with the statement that 'there is no need for strong trade unions to protect employees' working conditions and wages'. This is down from the corresponding figure for 1998 of 71 per cent. There is a significant gender difference in the responses to this question, with 70 per cent of males expressing their opposition (74 per cent in 1998) but only 58 per cent of females (68 per cent in 1998). This suggests that there may be a decline in the perceived need for union representation, particularly among female workers, making the union organising task even more difficult.

ATTITUDES TO JOBS AND WORKING TIME

Respondents to the 2000 Life and Times survey were asked a number of questions about their attitudes to work and their job (Table 5.2). When asked if they agree that 'a job is just a way of earning money – no more', there is a difference in the responses by gender, with 49 per cent of males agreeing compared with only 38 per cent of females. Asked if they agree that 'work is a person's most important activity', 36 per cent of males agree and 40 per cent disagree. The female responses differ with only 22 per cent saying that they agree and 53 per cent disagreeing. The differences in responses by gender to both questions are statistically significant. Work clearly plays a different role in the lives of females than it does in those of males.

When asked if they wanted to spend more time in a paid job the responses are similar across both gender and religion – about 16 per cent agree. This does not suggest any big demand by females, many of whom are part time, to work longer hours. When asked if they wanted to spend less time in a paid job, the response is similar by gender. However, there is a statistically significant difference by religion: 25 per cent of Protestants agree, compared with 34 per cent of Catholics and those of no religion. The Protestant work ethic still exists.

The ability to decide their times or days of work (flexitime) was considered to be either important or very important by 49 per cent of employees

Table 5.2   Attitudes to job by gender and religion (% agreeing)

	All	Male	Female	Catholic	Protestant	No religion
A job is just a way of earning money – no more	43	49	38	42	42	51
Work is a person's most important activity	29	36	22	25	29	36
Would like to spend more time in a paid job	16	15	17	14	17	20
Would like to spend less time in a paid job	29	28	28	34	25	34

Source: Life and Times survey 2000

Table 5.3 Importance of flexitime in a job (%)

	All	18–24	25–34	35–44	45–54	55–64	65+
Very important	12	12	14	12	15	10	8
Important	37	41	44	34	35	40	29
Neither	31	28	30	32	31	35	31
Not important	12	17	8	15	11	7	13
Not at all important	2	2	3	2	1	3	4
Other answer	6	2	1	6	8	5	15

Source: Life and Times survey 2000

who took part in the 2000 Life and Times survey, with only 14 per cent considering it to be unimportant. Females give more emphasis to flexible working than males, but this difference is not statistically significant. This is perhaps surprising, given that 68 per cent of females say that they are mainly responsible for doing the general domestic duties like cleaning, cooking, washing and so on in their household, compared with 19 per cent of males. It may be that females have already achieved most of their desired work–life balance through part-time working, with 39 per cent of females working 30 or fewer hours. The emphasis on flexibility is strongest among respondents aged 25 to 34 years, the age group within which many people have young families. In this age group, 58 per cent think flexibility is either important or very important, and the differences between age groups are statistically significant. This suggests that the desire for family-friendly policies on working time is related to age (Table 5.3).

WORKING CONDITIONS AND WORK MOTIVATION

Somewhat surprisingly, there does not appear to have been much change in working conditions over the last decade. The proportion of respondents reporting that they find work stressful has remained fairly constant since 1989. In the 2000 Life and Times survey, approximately 30 per cent of the workforce report that they find work stressful always or often (Table 5.4). Around two in five (37 per cent) of those in employment arrive home from work exhausted always or often, a slightly smaller proportion than 41 per cent in 1989 (Table 5.5).

There are statistically significant differences between Catholics and Protestants, with 36 per cent of Catholics reporting they often or always find their work stressful, compared with 26 per cent of Protestants; 43 per cent of Catholics report that they are always or often exhausted on returning home from work, compared with 33 per cent of Protestants.

Table 5.4   Find work stressful (%)

	All		Catholic	Protestant	No religion
	1989	2000		2000	
Always/often	29	31	36	26	34
Sometimes	48	46	42	48	46
Hardly ever/never	23	24	22	26	16
Other answer	–	1	–	1	4

Sources: Northern Ireland Social Attitudes survey 1989; Life and Times survey 2000

Table 5.5   Come home from work exhausted (%)

	All		Catholic	Protestant	No religion
	1989	2000		2000	
Always/often	41	37	43	33	36
Sometimes	44	50	47	54	40
Hardly ever/never	15	12	10	13	20
Other answer	–	1	–	1	4

Sources: Northern Ireland Social Attitudes survey 1989; Life and Times survey 2000

This may be related to the finding in Table 5.2 that a higher proportion of Catholics want to spend less time in a paid job.

Despite this, in 2000, 83 per cent of respondents in employment are satisfied in their job, a figure that has remained fairly constant since 1989. Females and Catholics are more satisfied in their jobs than males and Protestants. Only 5 per cent of females and 3 per cent of Catholics express dissatisfaction with their jobs compared with 12 per cent of males and 8 per cent of Protestants.

More dramatically, there does appear to have been a collapse of work motivation over the last decade (Table 5.6). In 1989, 58 per cent of those in employment reported that they make a point of doing the best work they can, even if it sometimes does interfere with the rest of their lives. By 2000, this figure has fallen to 36 per cent. In 1989, 8 per cent of respondents said that they only worked as hard as they had to. By 2000 this figure has risen to 13 per cent. This drop in work effort is so large one can only speculate that it may have been caused by something outside the workplace. This issue needs further research. Protestants show somewhat different work attitudes from Catholics, as do males from females, but these are relatively minor differences compared with the massive deterioration in the overall attitude to hard work since 1989. In 2000, just over

Table 5.6   How hard respondent works at their job (% agreeing)

	All		Catholic	Protestant	Male	Female
	1989	2000		2000		
Only work as hard as I have to	8	13	12	9	12	13
Work hard but not so it interferes with life	30	49	53	49	46	51
Do best work even if it does interfere with life	58	36	33	38	39	33

Sources: Northern Ireland Social Attitudes survey 1989; Life and Times survey 2000

a half of employees (56 per cent) agree that they are willing to work harder than they have to, to help the firm or organisation they work for succeed.

EMPLOYMENT MANAGEMENT

The predominant trend since 1979 has been the consolidation of managerial control as employers pursue competitive advantage in an increasingly global economy. Unilateral rule-making by managers, rather than joint regulation with trade unions, has become much more widespread. According to the LFS (2001), only 45 per cent of employees in Northern Ireland have their pay influenced by a collective agreement, although this is considerably higher than the United Kingdom average figure of 30 per cent. While 75 per cent of public sector workers in Northern Ireland have their pay and conditions affected by collective agreements, this applies to only one in four (25 per cent) of private sector workers.

There is a shortage of information on workplace representation and collective bargaining arrangements in Northern Ireland. However, it is possible to take the results of the 1998 Workplace Employment Relations survey (WERS) conducted in Britain, and assume that the overall trends have been experienced in Northern Ireland, even if not to the same extent. According to WERS, only 45 per cent of workplaces recognised trade unions in 1998, reflecting a further fall in recognition throughout the 1990s (Millward, Bryson and Forth, 2000). Of these, only three-quarters had a local union representative, and only 11 per cent of non-union workplaces had worker representatives. The absence of a union presence in the workplace has resulted in the loss of a collective voice, while also probably weakening the individual employee voice. Moreover, even in unionised workplaces WERS noted that in a significant proportion of workplaces with recognition, management was not supportive of a union role in joint negotiations, or even joint consultations, preferring instead to consult directly with employees rather than trade unions.

We would expect union recognition to be less prevalent in the smaller private sector workplaces that are typical of Northern Ireland. Reid, Morrow, Kelly and McCartan (2002) found that only 10 per cent of family businesses with 20 to 100 employees in Northern Ireland negotiated with trade unions on pay and conditions. The corresponding figure for non-family businesses in the same size range was 28 per cent.

This lack of local trade union representation and its decline over time helps to explain the growing use of legal enactment to resolve individual complaints, as well as the resulting increase in the individual conciliation cases being dealt with by the LRA and the increased number of cases coming before industrial tribunals. The LRA received 5,420 applications for individual conciliation in the year ending March 2002 (not including 548 fair employment applications) (LRA, 2002). These covered applications under jurisdictions such as unfair dismissal (1,952 cases), wages orders (862 cases), sex discrimination (781 cases), breach of contract (684 cases), other employment rights (545 cases), equal pay (292 cases), disability discrimination (175 cases) and race discrimination (126 cases).

Despite these figures, relations in the workplace between management and employees in Northern Ireland are fairly satisfactory, with 70 per cent of respondents to the 2000 Life and Times survey saying relations are either very good or quite good (Table 5.7).

Approximately a half of respondents (49 per cent) to the 1999 Life and Times survey thought that there was little conflict between management and workers, while 41 per cent thought there was strong or very strong conflict between managers and workers. Females and Protestants were more likely to report conflict in their workplace than males or Catholics.

Table 5.7 Perception of management–employee relations (%)

	1990	2000
Very good	39	33
Quite good	48	37
Neither	–	17
Quite bad	7	6
Very bad	5	2
Other answer	–	5

Sources: Northern Ireland Social Attitudes survey 1990; Life and Times survey 2000

However, survey evidence suggests that relations in the workplace between workmates and colleagues are generally harmonious in Northern Ireland: 85 per cent of respondents to the 2000 Life and Times survey describe relations as being quite good or very good, with only 2 per cent describing them as quite bad.

INDUSTRIAL DISPUTES

The average number of working days lost in strikes and the number of stoppages in progress in the United Kingdom during the period 1996 to 2000 continued at the extremely low levels that have prevailed since the early 1990s. This parallels an international decline in industrial action in recent decades. This pattern has been reflected in Northern Ireland, where the average number of working days lost per thousand employees (all industries and services) from 1996 to 2000 was 21.4, almost exactly equal to the United Kingdom average of 21.2. While the Northern Ireland figure was higher than that of Wales at 14.8, it was much better than that of Scotland at 52.4 and better than that of the north east of England at 27.6 (Table 5.8). Over a half of the stoppages and three-quarters of the working days lost in Northern Ireland from 1996 to 2000 were in the manufacturing and transport, storage and communication sectors.

The low level of overt industrial conflict has been reflected in a sharp decline in the number of collective conciliation cases received by the LRA, with the agency's case load currently running at about one-third of the level of the early to mid-1990s.

In the spring/summer quarters of 2000, 2.1 per cent of employees were absent due to sickness in Northern Ireland, compared with a United Kingdom average of 2.8 per cent (National Statistics, LFS). The comparable figure for Scotland was 3.0 per cent. These figures may provide indirect confirmation that conflict in the workplace is relatively contained, despite the rise in industrial tribunal applications and the minority of employees

Table 5.8 Working days lost per 1,000 employees, all industries and services

	1996	1997	1998	1999	2000	Average 1996–2000
United Kingdom	55	10	11	10	20	21.2
Northern Ireland	35	23	6	10	33	21.4
Scotland	57	25	23	21	136	52.4
Wales	59	3	2	4	6	14.8
North east	84	36	9	3	6	27.6

Source: National Statistics, *Labour Market Trends* (2001a)

reporting bad relations between management and employees. However, findings from the 2000 Life and Times survey show that 7 per cent of those in employment were absent eleven or more days (not counting vacation) in the previous six months.

EARNINGS

Average weekly earnings of full-time employees in April 2000 were 12 per cent lower in Northern Ireland than the United Kingdom average (National Statistics, New Earnings survey). This may reflect the fact that relatively low productivity continues to be a problem in Northern Ireland with output per head continuing to lag some 20 per cent behind that in Britain, which in turn lags behind competitors such as the United States, Germany and France (Economic Development Forum, 2002). Earnings in Northern Ireland were lower for both males and females in every occupational group except in the personal and protective services (which includes security and prison staff), where male employees in particular earned more than in Britain.

The relative incidence of low pay among females working full time has been considerably reduced since the introduction of the national minimum wage in 1998. In April 1999, the proportion of males working full time in Northern Ireland earning less than £200 per week was 14.3 per cent, compared with a United Kingdom average of 8.1 per cent. The proportion of females working full time in Northern Ireland earning less than £200 was 28.4 per cent compared with 20.4 per cent in the United Kingdom. In contrast, in 1994, 36 per cent of females working full time in Northern Ireland earned less than £170 per week, compared with a United Kingdom average of 23.3 per cent.

EMPLOYMENT LEGISLATION

The world of employment has been revolutionised since 1980 and is now legally regulated to an extent that few would have anticipated. The Labour government has largely retained the employment and trade union legislation inherited from the previous Conservative administration. The restrictive trade union legislation of that period continues to contribute to the shifting of the balance of power in employment relations from trade unions to management.

The main initiatives introduced by the current Labour administration include the introduction of a statutory national minimum wage, the introduction of legislation on statutory trade union recognition for collective bargaining purposes and the introduction of a new alternative disputes procedure, together with a further extension of individual rights in employment, many of them aimed at promoting a more 'family-friendly' workplace.

The emphasis in employment policy has shifted from the resolution of disputes to the prevention of disputes and the spread of good practice. At the same time, the European Union influence on employment relations has continued to increase, with the United Kingdom signing up to the European Social Chapter in 1997. As a result, a number of European Directives such as the European Works Council Directive, and Directives on Working Time and Part-Time Workers, have become effective in Northern Ireland.

The introduction of the National Minimum Wage reflects an overdue recognition that collective bargaining could not be relied on to eliminate poverty wages in many sectors of the economy. The new statutory trade union recognition procedure provides a mechanism for establishing collective representation where a majority of the workforce desire it, but it is unlikely in the current climate that these procedures will lead to the widespread restoration of collective bargaining.

At the same time, society has become much more litigious, and there has been an increase in the number of lawyers earning a living from employment law. Employees are becoming much more aware of their individual rights in employment and are much more prepared to assert them in the prevailing 'claims' culture. Employers, in turn, are becoming more conscious of the need to have procedures in place, and of the need to adhere closely to them if they are to avoid costly damages. Equally, employers and unions are aware that collective action is also subject to strict legal regulation, so that procedures are again of paramount importance if expensive damages are to be avoided by unions engaging in industrial action.

This long-term trend towards the legal regulation of the employment relationship has had a number of effects. Firstly, it has been associated with an explosion of enquiries from individuals, trade unions and employers requesting information about their statutory rights. Secondly, it has resulted in a steady increase in the number of applications from individuals alleging that their statutory rights have been infringed. Thirdly, it has coincided with, and may have been partly responsible for, the long-term decline in collective representation and industrial action outlined above.

CONCLUSION

This chapter has painted a fairly favourable portrait of the current world of work. Employment has been expanding, unemployment has been falling (although long-term male unemployment still remains a problem), real wages have been rising and the worst aspects of low pay have been removed by the introduction of the statutory National Minimum Wage. While many employees, including three-quarters of those working in the private sector, are not represented by trade unions, they have more statutory rights at work. While the workforce is increasingly well skilled to prosper in the knowledge economy, there is still a major educational and training challenge to improve the position of those without any qualifications.

The major problem identified is one of work motivation. On the evidence from the Northern Ireland Social Attitudes surveys and the Life and Times surveys, the proportion of employees saying that they make a point of doing the best work they can, even if it sometimes interferes with the rest of their lives, has declined dramatically since 1989. At the same time, the proportion saying they only work as hard as they have to has risen. We can only speculate about the possible cause of this, but it has serious implications for the competitiveness of the economy.

The issue of work motivation highlights the urgency of the government's partnership agenda for employee involvement (DTI, 2002). To rekindle employee commitment and revitalise work effort there needs to be a concerted effort to involve employees more effectively in the running of their organisations.

REFERENCES

Boxall, P. and Purcell, J. (2003) *Strategy and Human Resource Management* (Basingstoke: Palgrave Macmillan).

Brown, W. (2000) 'Putting partnership into practice in Britain', *British Journal of Industrial Relations*, Vol. 38, No. 2, pp. 299–316.

Department of Trade and Industry (DTI) (2001) *Routes to Resolution: Improving Dispute Resolution in Britain* (London: DTI).

Department of Trade and Industry (DTI) (2002) *High Performance Workplaces. The Role of Employee Involvement in a Modern Economy* (London: DTI).

Economic Development Forum (2002) *Working Together for a Stronger Economy*, Annex 3, Table D (Belfast: GCAS).

Gaffikin, F. and Morrisey, M. (1990) *Northern Ireland: The Thatcher Years* (London: Zed).

Labour Relations Agency (LRA) (2002) *Annual Report and Accounts 2001–02* (Belfast: Labour Relations Agency).

Millward, N., Bryson, A. and Forth, J. (2000) *All Change at Work?* (London: Routledge).

National Statistics, Labour Force Surveys (LFS) <http://www.statistics.gov.uk/ssd/surveys/labour_force_survey.asp>.

National Statistics, New Earnings Surveys <http://www.statistics.gov.uk/StatBase/Product.asp?vlnk=647&More=Y>.

National Statistics (2001a) *Labour Market Trends*, June (London: The Stationery Office).

National Statistics (2001b) *Social Trends* (London: The Stationery Office).

Northern Ireland Certification Officer for Trade Unions and Employers' Associations, *Annual Reports* (Belfast: Certification Office for Trade Unions and Employers' Associations).

Northern Ireland Economic Research Centre (NIERC)/Oxford Economic Forecasting (2001) *Regional Economic Outlook, Autumn 2001* (Belfast: NIERC).

Reid, R., Morrow, T., Kelly, B. and McCartan, P. (2002) 'People management in SMEs: an analysis of human resource strategies in family and non-family businesses', *Journal of Small Business and Enterprise Development*, Vol. 9, No. 3, pp. 245–59.

6
Culture in Northern Ireland

Deirdre Heenan

Since the early 1990s there has been an upsurge of interest in the concept of culture in Northern Ireland. Mirfenderesky (2002) claimed that there is incessant talk about culture, cultural traditions, cultural symbolism, multiculturalism, cultural heritage, cultural tourism, cross-cultural relations and cultural celebrations. But what does the word 'culture' actually mean? It has been suggested that culture 'is probably the broadest concept of all those used in the historical social sciences. It embraces a very large range of connotations, and thereby it is the cause perhaps of the most difficulty' (Wallerstein, 1990, p. 31). Culture is a controversial and contested concept for which there is no widely accepted definition. According to the cultural theorist, Raymond Williams (1976) it is one of the two or three most complicated words in the English language. Indeed, such is the difficulty and confusion surrounding the term that the poet Hanns Johst commented, 'whenever I hear the word culture, I release the safety catch on my pistol' (cited in Nolan, 1998, p.146).

Despite the confusion surrounding the term culture, it features strongly in the literature and debates on the conflict in Northern Ireland. The existence of different cultural traditions in Northern Ireland has resulted in volumes of work on cultural heritage and diversity. Somewhat surprisingly therefore, given the importance attached to the concept of culture by those engaged in assessing the political situation in Northern Ireland, there has been little attempt to ascertain public perceptions of it. Reflecting the heightened profile given to the area of culture, as illustrated by the creation of a Department for Culture, Arts and Leisure under the Good Friday Agreement, a module on culture, leisure and the arts was included in the 2001 Northern Ireland Life and Times survey. The main issues covered were perceptions of the term culture, participation in cultural activities and identification of barriers to participation. This chapter begins by briefly considering the use of the concept of culture in Northern Ireland. From this background, the main findings of the survey are then considered. As such the chapter provides an intriguing insight into the public's perceptions of culture and their participation in cultural activities.

CULTURE IN NORTHERN IRELAND

Traditionally the term culture has been associated with anthropology, although more recently it has been used to inform a wide range of social sciences. Featherstone has argued that there is a fundamental difference in the way anthropologists use the term and the way it is viewed by other social scientists:

> for many social sciences, culture has been seen as something on the periphery of the field as, for example, we find in conceptualisations, which wish to restrict it to the study of the arts. Even when this view became extended to incorporate the study of popular culture and every-day [*sic*] life, culture was still regarded by many as esoteric and epiphe-nomenal. Culture was … regarded as readily circumscribed; something derivative which was there to be explained. (1992, p. vii)

For sociologists, culture refers to the beliefs of the society and their symbolic representation through creative activities. A symbol can be thought of as a representation such as a painting or a sculpture. Culture can be best understood by distinguishing between beliefs, which are the content of the culture, and creative activities, which express this content in actions or words (Fulcher and Scott, 1999).

Within the context of Northern Ireland the term culture has often gone hand in hand with politics. In much of the existing literature, culture has not been associated with aesthetics or anthropology, but has been synony-mous with politics and identity. Commenting on the bid by Belfast to become the European Capital of Culture in 2008, Gray (2002) suggested that the fundamental question of what is understood by culture was 'impossibly dangerous' in post-ceasefire Belfast where culture has been a focus of conflict and violence. Relative to other areas of the United Kingdom, Northern Ireland has a unique set of social, political and eco-nomic problems. Since the beginning of the most recent Troubles in 1969 the region has been characterised by sectarian violence, and widespread civil and political unrest. Many academic studies have relied on theories of identity and culture to explain this conflict. To a large extent, the term culture has been highjacked by academics to explain the deep divisions that exist in Northern Ireland. The word is invariably associated with sectarianism, violence, divisions and differences.

It has been suggested that the conflict in Northern Ireland has persisted because the population lack the cultural tolerance and maturity to live with each other (Ruane and Todd, 1991). In this cultural approach, the abnor-mality of Northern Irish political culture is the source of the violence.

The expectations, values, norms and attitudes of the two communities in Northern Ireland are in stark contrast to contemporary cultural trends. To some people 'the culture of Northern Ireland' is simply shorthand for the bigotry, intransigence and religious intolerance illustrated by Orange parades and, until November 2001, the ban on members of the police force from joining the Gaelic Athletic Association. According to this cultural interpretation, the conflict persists in Northern Ireland because neither community is willing to compromise: Unionists want an entirely British Northern Ireland, while nationalists want an entirely Irish Ireland (Daly, 1988).

In response to calls to improve community relations and reduce religious discrimination, the Central Community Relations Unit was established in 1987 by central government in Northern Ireland. Such was the importance attached to issues of cultural diversity that a formal sub-committee of this unit, entitled the Cultural Traditions Group, was set up with the aim of promoting a constructive debate about the different cultural traditions in Northern Ireland. The Cultural Traditions Group was involved in considering the roles that could be played by the visual media, the arts, museums, drama and language in creating a society where cultural diversity is celebrated and welcomed. Particular emphasis was placed on young people and the importance of education in promoting mutual understanding. The Cultural Traditions Group ensured that culture was an issue at the forefront of political discussions in Northern Ireland, through a series of publications, events and conferences. Much of the work of the group focused on whether or not cultural pluralism was feasible in Northern Ireland or if divisions meant that each group ascribed to its own exclusive culture (Bardon, 1998; Glendinning, 1998).

WHAT DOES CULTURE MEAN TO PEOPLE IN NORTHERN IRELAND?

When respondents to the 2001 Life and Times survey were asked to describe, in their own words, what culture meant to them, the wide range of responses indicates that culture is indeed difficult to define and means different things to different people. However, for a sizeable majority of respondents, it is apparent that culture is associated with 'high culture' as the largest category of response is 'arts/theatre/museums/music/dance/books/painting', which accounts for almost a half of the total responses (49 per cent). Popular culture, such as pop concerts and watching television, do not feature significantly in descriptions of culture.

Interestingly, the more controversial aspects of culture – such as marching on the Twelfth of July or Irish history – are mentioned by relatively few of the respondents. The preoccupation with the political aspects of culture in the literature on Northern Ireland is not reflected in the responses.

As Table 6.1 shows, when the respondents were given a list of events and asked which they considered to be cultural activities, the association with high culture is again apparent. Museums top the list, followed by visiting natural heritage sites like the Giant's Causeway and going to the theatre. Going to the cinema is the activity that is least likely to be described as cultural. There is some differentiation by respondents between books that are less popular and those which are deemed to be 'highbrow', such as works by Charles Dickens. Authors such as Maeve Binchy and John Grisham, whose works have sold in millions, are considered to be cultural by only 25 per cent of respondents, compared with 40 per cent who believe that reading less popular books by authors such as Charles Dickens is cultural. As Table 6.2 shows, support for the contention that reading less popular books by authors such as Charles Dickens is cultural is significantly higher among respondents in the professional and managerial groups compared with those who are partly skilled or unskilled (47 per cent and 29 per cent respectively).

Table 6.1 Activities respondents would describe as cultural (% saying yes)

Going to visit a museum	77
Going to visit an attraction like the Giant's Causeway	71
Going to the theatre	66
Going to a play in a local community centre	46
Reading less popular books by authors like Charles Dickens	40
Going to visit the W5 centre at the Odyssey in Belfast*	26
Reading popular books by authors like John Grisham, Maeve Binchy or Agatha Christie	25
Going to the cinema	21

* W5 is an interactive science discovery centre

Table 6.2 Activities respondents would describe as cultural, by social class (% saying yes)

	Professional/ managerial	Skilled non-manual	Skilled manual	Partly/ unskilled manual
Reading less popular books by authors like Charles Dickens	47	46	30	29
Going to the cinema	28	23	17	18
Going to the theatre	75	71	59	54

Moreover, those in the higher social classes are more likely to consider going to the cinema and theatre as a cultural activity than those in the lower social classes. When the findings were disaggregated by age, it is apparent that younger people are more likely to describe going to W5 in the Odyssey arena as cultural than those in the older age groups. This could be due to the fact that the Odyssey is a relatively new attraction and older respondents may be unfamiliar with its attractions. Respondents' gender makes little difference to their opinions.

PARTICIPATION IN CULTURAL EVENTS

Respondents were asked whether they regularly do anything in their leisure time that is to do with culture. Remarkably, only one in five (21 per cent) claim that they do, and there is striking consistency among respondents in terms of age, gender and religion in relation to this. These activities range from watching football to amateur dramatics, although the most popular is 'go to museums/art galleries/theatre or concerts'.

The survey then explored how important a range of activities is to respondents within their own leisure time. As might be expected, participation in sport is more important for men than women. Just over half (53 per cent) of all men say that it is either very or quite important compared with 23 per cent of women. Also, predictably, participation in sport is more important for 18- to 24-year-olds than for older respondents.

Respondents in the higher social class groups attach more importance to participation in cultural events than those in the lower social class groups. As Table 6.3 shows, 43 per cent of those in the professional and managerial classes compared with only 18 per cent of those in the partly and unskilled manual classes say that taking part in cultural events is important to them. In his study on cultural production and consumption, Bourdieu (1984) noted not only that people's taste varies significantly by their social class but also that social classes reproduce these differences. Elite groups took steps to ensure that 'cultural capital' was passed on to

Table 6.3 Importance of participation in cultural events, by social class (%)

	Professional/ managerial	Skilled non-manual	Skilled manual	Partly/ unskilled manual
Important	43	29	24	18
Neither	14	15	16	11
Not important	42	54	57	69
Don't know	2	2	3	3

Table 6.4   Importance of participation in church activities, by religion (%)

	Catholic	Protestant	All
Very important	11	22	15
Quite important	26	30	26
Neither important nor unimportant	9	12	11
Not very important	24	14	19
Not at all important	29	21	29
Don't know	1	1	1

their children as this was considered to be important for their future success. As a result, cultural inequalities were continually reproduced within societies.

IMPORTANCE OF CHURCH ACTIVITIES

Many commentators have noted that levels of church attendance are significantly higher in Northern Ireland than in other parts of the United Kingdom. Brewer stated that 'what has distinguished Northern Irish Christians from their British coreligionists in the past is the higher numbers of them who live out their faith in religious observance' (2002, p. 7). One might assume, therefore, that participation in church activities would also be a feature of the lives of the people of Northern Ireland. Table 6.4 shows the importance attached to taking part in church activities by both Protestants and Catholics. Overall, just 15 per cent of respondents describe their participation in church activities as very important, with a further 26 per cent describing it as quite important. The relatively large proportion who say that church activities are not very important or not at all important may also be related to the assertion that religious observance is something that people do either very regularly or very irregularly (Bruce and Alderdice, 1993). As Table 6.4 indicates, there is a marked difference on the basis of religion among those who consider that taking part in church activities is a very important part of their own leisure time. Twice as many Protestants (22 per cent) as Catholics (11 per cent) consider that taking part in church activities is a very important part of their leisure time. While there is little variation by gender, it is perhaps unsurprising that the percentage of those who considered church activities very or quite important increased with the age of the respondent.

MORE OR LESS CULTURE

Since 2000, cultural activities in Northern Ireland have had a relatively high profile. This may be due to a number of factors such as Belfast's bid to become European Capital of Culture 2008, which attracted widespread media attention during 2001. In addition, the establishment of a Department of Culture, Arts and Leisure under the Good Friday Agreement meant that, for the first time, Northern Ireland had a government minister promoting cultural activities. It is interesting to note that, among respondents to the Life and Times survey, there is a general perception that Northern Ireland offers more cultural events and attractions than it used to: 51 per cent of respondents believe that compared with two years ago, Northern Ireland offers more cultural events and attractions (Table 6.5). Of those respondents who believe that Northern Ireland offers more cultural events and attractions than it used to, 95 per cent agree that this increase has generally been a good thing for people in Northern Ireland. Over a half of respondents (56 per cent) think it is positive as it brings people from different religions together. Table 6.6 shows that a similar proportion (54 per cent) feels it is a good thing as it brings people together socially.

Catholics (63 per cent) are more positive about the cross-community benefit than Protestants (55 per cent), while the latter are more likely to say that the increase in cultural activities brings people together socially (44 per cent and 61 per cent respectively).

Respondents were asked how much they and their families have benefited from the increase in cultural events and activities. As Table 6.7 shows, opinion is split; around one-fifth of respondents (19 per cent) feel they have benefited a lot, while a similar proportion (21 per cent) feel they have not benefited at all. So who do they think is benefiting? There is a general feeling that some groups have benefited more than others; 53 per cent of respondents agree with this. Of these, almost three-quarters (71 per cent)

Table 6.5 Change in amount of cultural events and attractions in last 2 years (%)

More	51
Less	3
Same	24
Don't know	22

Table 6.6 In what ways has the increase in cultural activities been a good thing? (%)

	Catholic	Protestant	All
Brings people from different religions together	63	55	56
Brings people together socially	44	61	54

Table 6.7 Benefit to respondents from the increase in cultural events and attractions (%)

A lot	19
A little	37
Hardly any	22
Not at all	21

Table 6.8 Reasons for non-participation in cultural events (%)

I'm not interested in cultural events or attractions	38
I am interested but I haven't got time to go to many of these things	30
If cultural events and attractions were cheaper I would probably go to more	20
I miss many of these things because I don't hear about them in time	17
Many of these cultural events or attractions just aren't really for people like me	15
I don't drive so I can't get to many cultural events or attractions	10
These things are difficult to get to because so many are based in Belfast	10
My health problems or disability makes it difficult to get to these things	7
I'm too old to be going to these things	7
(None of the statements apply to the respondent)	10

Note: respondents could identify more than one reason

gave a rather vague 'people who are interested in/like that kind of thing' response, and it is therefore difficult to draw conclusions about respondents' views on which groups have benefited the most.

BARRIERS TO PARTICIPATION

In order to explore why people do not participate in cultural events, respondents were given a set of cards and asked to decide which of the statements on the cards applied to them. Remarkably, as Table 6.8 shows, 38 per cent of respondents report that they are not interested in cultural events or attractions. Obviously this reported lack of interest depends on the earlier question of what is perceived to be cultural. However, almost one-third of respondents (30 per cent) would like to be involved in cultural activities but cannot afford the time. It could be surmised that for many respondents, who are struggling to meet the demands of work and family, going out to cultural events may be perceived as more of an effort than a pleasurable leisure-time activity.

Cost constraints are mentioned by 20 per cent of respondents. It seems likely that high costs are associated with art events such as visiting the Opera House or the Waterfront Hall in Belfast. For those who are unemployed or surviving on a low income, the amount of money required may be a deterrent. Participating in cultural events can be expensive when the costs of refreshments and travelling are taken into account. In Northern Ireland the vast majority of cultural venues are located in Belfast, so for those living outside the greater Belfast area participating in cultural events may require significant time and financial commitments.

PROMOTION OF CULTURAL EVENTS

When asked who they believe is responsible for encouraging people to take part in cultural events and visit cultural attractions, just 14 per cent of respondents suggest that it is mainly the government's responsibility to promote cultural attractions (Table 6.9). Given that 39 per cent agree it is not the government's responsibility to encourage participation in cultural events, it seems that many respondents view cultural activities as a matter of personal choice. People will become involved in what interests them, which may not necessarily be what is promoted by government.

Despite the fact that the majority of respondents do not consider the promotion of cultural activities as the concern of government, Belfast City Council sees itself as having a key role in relation to the cultural development of the city. A core aim of the council's development plan is to increase access to, and participation in, the arts and heritage throughout the city, in the recognition that creative activity is an essential element in improving quality of life. The council has expressed a desire to play a more proactive role targeting resources in a way that is in the wider public interest. It states that 'we are embracing an inclusive idea of culture – as an expression of identity, as a source of inspiration and learning and as a force for personal and social development' (Belfast City Council, 2002, p. 2). Yet in 2002, Belfast City Council cut its funding for major arts organisations from £762,000 to £600,000 without any consultation. This 21 per cent cut in the budget meant that some smaller groups had to close and others were forced to radically rethink their plans.

Table 6.9 Role of government in encouraging cultural participation (%)

It is mainly the government's responsibility to encourage people to take part in cultural events and visit cultural attractions	14
It is partly the government's responsibility to encourage people to take part in cultural events and visit cultural attractions	34
It is not the government's responsibility to encourage people to take part in cultural events and visit cultural attractions	39
Other	1
Don't know	13

The location of cultural events within Northern Ireland has historically been problematic due to the identification of areas with particular religions. Within Belfast, traditionally the city centre and university area are perceived to be neutral venues and consequently cultural activities have been concentrated in these areas. In recent years, however, there have been moves to widen access to cultural events and encourage community networks to develop their own activities, which focus on local issues. The aim of this promotion and facilitation of locally based events such as the West Belfast Festival and the Greater Shankill Festival is to enable citizens to celebrate identity and cultural diversity. New strategies are focused on empowering local communities to celebrate their own heritage and traditions. As Mayo (2000) has noted, community arts and the media can be used to facilitate more empowering processes of community representation and participation from the bottom up.

In his study of the community arts sector in Belfast, Matarosso (1998) found substantial evidence that it made a positive contribution. It was seen as improving the self-confidence and employability of participants. He concluded that such projects were also creating opportunities for cross-community cooperation. However, while there is no doubt that community-based festivals have the potential to unite rather than divide in Northern Ireland, things are rarely straightforward. Wilson and Gallagher (2002) lament the fact that a dichotomy based on social class developed in Belfast in the 1990s between a festival based in the university area and targeted at an elite audience and a community festival in west Belfast organised by the working class aimed at a working-class audience. They contrast this with the Galway Arts Festival, which is an international cosmopolitan affair and is an important tourist attraction.

CONCLUSION

What then can be concluded from this first look at public perceptions of culture? There appears to be very little support for the assumption within much of the literature in Northern Ireland that the concept of culture is inextricably linked with the conflict that has characterised the area. For the majority of the population the word culture conjures up visions of theatre, opera and ballet. Popular culture such as watching television is not generally considered to be cultural. There is overwhelming support for the contention that cultural activities are beneficial to the community.

Unsurprisingly people in the higher social classes are more likely to be involved in cultural events and are more likely to see them as important. The fact that perceptions of what is cultural are similar regardless of age, gender and religion is striking. The findings from the Life and Times survey reported in this chapter provide an important starting point for further, more detailed, research on what culture means in this society. Given the contested nature of space in Northern Ireland it also raises a wider set of questions about the inherent difficulties of locally based cultural festivals and the limitations of 'top-down' cultural strategies.

REFERENCES

Bardon, J. (1998) 'Cultural routes: ways of approaching diversity in cultural traditions in Northern Ireland' in M. Crozier and R. Froggatt (eds) *Cultural Traditions in Northern Ireland* (Belfast: Institute of Irish Studies) pp. 13–22.

Belfast City Council (2002) *Culture and Arts: The Spirit of the City* (Belfast: Belfast City Council).

Bourdieu, P. (1984) *Distinction* (London: Routledge).

Brewer, J.D. (2002) 'Are there any Christians in Northern Ireland?' in Ann Marie Gray, Katrina Lloyd, Paula Devine, Gillian Robinson and Deirdre Heenan (eds) *Social Attitudes in Northern Ireland: The Eight Report* (London: Pluto Press) pp. 22–38.

Bruce, S. and Alderdice, F. (1993) 'Religious belief and behaviour' in Peter Stringer and Gillian Robinson (eds) *Social Attitudes in Northern Ireland: The Third Report, 1992–1993* (Belfast: Blackstaff Press) pp. 5–20.

Daly, C. (1988) 'Towards a new society in which every person has a place', paper presented at a conference, Northern Ireland: Finding a Way Forward, Ballycastle, 8 October.

Featherstone, M. (1992) 'Preface cultural theory and cultural change: an introduction' in M. Featherstone (ed.) *Cultural Theory and Cultural Change* (London: Routledge) pp. vii–viii.

Fulcher, J. and Scott, J. (1999) *Sociology* (Oxford: Oxford University Press).

Glendinning, W. (1998) 'Diversity: an advantage or disadvantage?' in M. Crozier and R. Froggatt (eds) *Cultural Traditions in Northern Ireland* (Belfast: Institute of Irish Studies) pp. 122–7.

Gray, J. (2002) 'City of culture: we mean it literally', *Variant*, Vol. 2, No. 16, Winter, p. 38.

Matarosso, F. (1998) *Vital Signs – Mapping Community Arts in Belfast* (Stroud: Comedia).

Mayo, M. (2000) *Cultures, Communities, Identities: Cultural Strategies for Participation and Empowerment* (Basingstoke: Palgrave).

Mirfenderesky, J. (2002) 'Culture is what people do, not what they should do', *Fortnight*, November, pp. 22–5.

Nolan, S. (1998) 'Chairman's closing remarks' in M. Crozier and R. Froggatt (eds) *Cultural Traditions in Northern Ireland* (Belfast: Institute of Irish Studies) pp. 146–7.

Ruane, J. and Todd, J. (1991) 'Why can't you get along with each other? Culture, structure and the Northern Ireland conflict' in E. Hughes (ed.) *Culture and Politics in Northern Ireland 1960–1990* (Buckingham: Open University Press) pp. 27–43.

Wallerstein, I. (1990) 'Culture as the ideological battlefield of the modern world-system' in *Theory, Culture and Society*, Vol. 7, Nos 2–3, June, pp. 31–55.

Williams, R. (1976) *Keywords: A Vocabulary of Culture and Society* (London: Fontana).

Wilson, R. and Gallagher, A. (2002) 'Sharing versus sectarianism: Belfast case study', paper presented at the Council of Europe conference in Frankfurt-am-der-Oder, December.

7

Making a Difference? Public Attitudes to Devolution

Roger MacGinty

In the final quarter of 2001 the Northern Ireland Executive launched the draft of its second Programme for Government and engaged in an extensive consultation exercise to ascertain perceived needs among key audiences. Reviewing the first Programme for Government (2001–2002), First Minister David Trimble noted that 'one year on we can see that the devolved Government is delivering open and accountable government for the people ... we have shown that we can make a difference' (Wilford, 2002). Commending the 2002–2003 Programme to the Assembly, Deputy First Minister Mark Durkan noted the public desire for a prioritisation of health and social issues. According to Durkan, 'the Executive are committed to ensuring that their plans ... are not merely good intentions' (Hansard, 24 September 2001). While acknowledging continuing political difficulties, the Ulster Unionist Party's (UUP) Sir Reg Empey told the Assembly that 'there is much of a positive nature to report' and went on to state that 'we know now that by working together we can – and do – make a real difference' (Hansard, 24 September 2001).

Clearly key members of the Executive felt that devolution was making a difference. But was this view shared among Northern Ireland's public? The fieldwork for the Northern Ireland Life and Times survey took place from October to December 2001, at precisely the time that the first Programme for Government was being replaced by the second Programme. Survey respondents would be able to make their judgements on the devolved government's stated aims and delivery of those aims. By the time the second Programme for Government was introduced to the Assembly in September 2001, 37 out of 200 pledges in the first Programme had been fully implemented (Wilford, 2002). The commitments made in the first Programme would remain relevant and would be built upon in the second Programme. A number of initiatives had already been introduced – for example, free public transport for the elderly – or were under discussion, for example, long-term care for the elderly

(Hansard, 27 February 2001). Respondents would have at least some evidence upon which to assess the Assembly as an instrument of government and a provider of services in the context of devolution.

It is worth noting that a year is a short period upon which to judge the impact of a legislative programme. Moreover, Northern Ireland's devolution experience was subject to extreme turbulence, with political attention often devoted to the hangovers of entrenched political violence: continuing paramilitary violence and retention of arms, policing reform, and the cancer of sectarian violence. Indeed, the latter phenomenon experienced an upsurge in 2001, and the survey fieldwork coincided with the Holy Cross school dispute in north Belfast. The dispute, ostensibly concerning the route Catholic children and their parents took to a school in a Protestant area, reflected deeper tensions of social exclusion with a sectarian twist. The broader political context was already complicated: the 1998 Good Friday Agreement had attempted to put constitutional issues to bed for the medium term through the introduction of a sophisticated consociational accord that prioritised local powersharing devolution (Wilford, 2001b; MacGinty and Darby, 2002). The Agreement was augmented by a range of guarantees aimed at allaying the fears of Catholic nationalists and Protestant unionists (Bell, 2001). A complex institutional architecture connected Northern Ireland's Assembly with other institutions in the British Isles. A poisonous atmosphere characterised the implementation of the Agreement and could not hide a fundamental distrust between nationalists and unionists. Many unionists felt that nationalists had got 'a better deal' as a result of the Agreement and doubtless this informed their view of the operation of devolved government. Indeed, Northern Ireland Secretary of State, Dr John Reid (2001), recognised the dangers of Protestant alienation and warned that Northern Ireland should not become a 'cold place' for Protestants.

Abnormality characterised Northern Ireland's devolved government. The Democratic Unionist Party (DUP) refused to sit in the Executive with Sinn Féin. The relationship between Seamus Mallon, the original Deputy First Minister, and David Trimble, the First Minister, was notoriously poor. Sinn Féin was suing David Trimble over his refusal to allow its ministers to participate in the North–South Ministerial Council. Attempts to exclude parties and individuals from the Assembly chamber were commonplace. Yet, against this unpromising backdrop, one astute observer noted – with good reason – that 'the Assembly achieved something approximating to normality in this period' (Wilford, 2002). Indeed, the BBC reviewing the 2 December 1999 to 31 March 2002 period found that devolution had seen 125 plenary meetings of the Assembly, the submission of 8,477 questions for written answers, 1,168 committee meetings, the production of 71 committee reports, and the introduction of 34 Bills (BBC News Online, 2 December 2002). These things are relative, but the Assembly and Executive were leaving a footprint on Northern Ireland. A legislative programme had been initiated. Two budgets had been introduced. New systems for local governance were being put in place and an extensive series of consultation exercises with non-governmental organisations (NGOs) and others had broadened the ambit of government far beyond that achieved under direct rule. Indeed a senior member of the Social Democratic and Labour Party, Eddie McGrady, warned of 'consultation fatigue', 'paralysis by analysis' and a seeming fear of reaching decisions in the health sector (Wilford, 2001a). The devolved institutions were the recipients of substantial local media coverage, some of it the result of predictable political hubris and 'hissy-fits', but much of it the result of public policy initiatives and consultation. In short, Life and Times survey respondents had some evidence of the operation of devolved government upon which to base their answers.

NORTHERN IRELAND'S ROLE IN A DEVOLVED UNITED KINGDOM

Life and Times survey respondents were asked if they thought that New Labour's devolution project in Wales, Scotland and Northern Ireland strengthened or weakened the United Kingdom. While 21 per cent say that the United Kingdom was stronger after devolution, 17 per cent feel that it was weaker (Table 7.1). Protestants are more likely than Catholics to see devolution as corrosive to the Union (25 per cent and 8 per cent respectively), but perhaps we could have expected more Protestant concern at the constitutional implications of devolution. The constitutional dangers of devolution, and the peace process in general, were a major plank of public pronouncements from the DUP. A DUP leaflet for the May 1998 referendum on the Agreement warned that a 'yes' vote would 'wreck the Union' and lead to 'an embryonic united Ireland government'.

The most common response to the question of the impact of devolution on the Union is that devolution made no difference; this answer accounted for 47 per cent of Catholics and 53 per cent of Protestants. This suggests

Table 7.1   Effect of devolution on the United Kingdom (%)

	Protestant	Catholic	All
Strengthened it	17	27	21
Weakened it	25	8	17
Made no difference	47	53	50
Don't know	12	12	13

Table 7.2 Effect of devolution on the United Kingdom,
by how people voted in the 1998 referendum (%)

	Voted yes	*Voted no*
Strengthened it	26	13
Weakened it	15	36
Made no difference	48	47
Don't know	10	4

a widely held view that disconnects devolution from a constitutional reordering of the United Kingdom, and instead views it in more minimalist terms as a reappropriation of functional responsibilities.

When broken down according to those who said they voted 'yes' or 'no' in the 1998 referendum on the Good Friday Agreement, 36 per cent of 'no' voters – more than double the figure for all respondents – say that devolution weakened the Union (Table 7.2). Yet even among 'no' voters, a plurality (that is, the largest proportion) – 47 per cent – say that devolution made no difference in terms of weakening or strengthening the Union. 'Yes' voters display a similar equanimity on the constitutional implications of devolution, with 48 per cent saying that devolution made no difference.

Respondents were then asked if the Northern Ireland Assembly gave Northern Ireland a stronger or weaker voice in the United Kingdom. In theory, devolution gave Northern Ireland the opportunity to develop a distinct identity within the United Kingdom's changing constitutional geometry. Local ministers empowered by local mandates would be able to press Northern Ireland's case in Westminster and Whitehall, and in relation to the other devolved institutions across the United Kingdom. Under direct rule, internal government discussion on Northern Ireland was subsumed within the Cabinet and was rarely aired other than to give a united response. Under devolution, however, Northern Ireland would have its own government that could press Northern Ireland's case. Prime Minister Tony Blair, addressing the Welsh Assembly, noted how devolution had given Wales a 'strong voice' and caused envy in the English regions.[1] Was this the case in Northern Ireland?

The findings from the Life and Times survey show that 42 per cent of respondents say that the Assembly gave Northern Ireland a stronger voice in the United Kingdom (Table 7.3). Encouragingly for those charged with representing Stormont's case in the wider United Kingdom, only 11 per cent think that the Assembly gave Northern Ireland a weaker voice, but 38 per cent think that the Assembly made no difference. Part of the problem may have been identified by the Director of Democratic Dialogue,

Table 7.3   Effect of the Assembly on Northern Ireland's voice in
the United Kingdom (%)

	Protestant	Catholic	All
Stronger voice	34	55	42
Weaker voice	16	5	11
Making no difference	43	32	38
Don't know	8	8	9

Robin Wilson (2002a), who noted that 'the administration has no corporate character ... and no ethos of collective responsibility'. In other words, the task of giving Northern Ireland a stronger voice in the United Kingdom may have been complicated by an acutely divided Executive, many of whose members were united only in a desire never to sing from the same hymnal as their ministerial colleagues. It is also interesting to speculate whether the relatively strong perception of the Northern Ireland Assembly's ability to make itself heard in the United Kingdom was actually shared in Wales, Scotland and England, and the political institutions within those territories. The Northern Ireland Assembly's ability to make the headlines across the United Kingdom was usually for the wrong reasons and cannot be viewed as giving the region a stronger voice in the United Kingdom. Furthermore, the Scottish and Welsh devolved institutions had a comparative advantage over Northern Ireland in that members of their Executives could employ internal Labour Party networks for centre–periphery and periphery–periphery communication.

Responses to this and other questions are interesting in that they do not suggest widely held negative perceptions of the experience of devolution. Nor do many of the survey responses point towards the widespread Protestant dissatisfaction that was a persistent theme in unionist political discourse. Certainly the survey findings reveal that Catholics tend to hold more positive views of the Assembly than Protestants. But respondents – and particularly Protestants – are much more likely to say that devolution was 'making no difference' than to express an unequivocal negative opinion. This may be a reflection of the relative infancy of devolution and the fact that people needed more time and evidence upon which to base their assessments. It also suggests that many people were willing to give devolution a chance rather than immediately reaching negative conclusions.

Respondents were asked to identify the institutions that had, and ought to have, the most influence over how Northern Ireland was run. A slim majority (51 per cent) say that the United Kingdom government at Westminster had most say, with 28 per cent opting for the Northern Ireland Assembly (Table 7.4). There is little difference between Catholic

Table 7.4   Influence of institutions over the way Northern Ireland is run (%)

	Has most influence			Ought to have most influence		
	Protestant	*Catholic*	*All*	*Protestant*	*Catholic*	*All*
Northern Ireland Assembly	29	28	28	61	74	65
UK government at Westminster	50	53	51	24	7	17

and Protestant opinion. But on the question of which institution *should* hold most power over the way Northern Ireland is run, a strong majority – 65 per cent – opt for the Assembly, as against 17 per cent for Westminster. While comfortable majorities of both Catholics and Protestants favour the Assembly, Catholic support is stronger. Just under a quarter of Protestants (24 per cent) and only 7 per cent of Catholics award primacy to the 'Mother of all Parliaments' at Westminster. Other options, such as local government or the European Union, were included in the survey and attracted minimal support. The findings in Table 7.4 can be taken as a public willingness to see more power devolved to Northern Ireland. The opportunity for the extension of devolution already exists; a lengthy list of issues currently rests within the Whitehall domain. These 'reserved matters', ranging from public order and consumer safety to the regulation of activities in outer space, may be devolved at a future date. 'Excepted matters', on the other hand, are regarded as permanently under Whitehall control and include national security and taxation.

The popular inclination to see more power devolved to Northern Ireland is a remarkable public endorsement of a relatively untested form of government that had a chequered and brief history at the time of the survey. To a certain extent it can be interpreted as a profound dissatisfaction with direct rule and an anticipation of the potential of devolution. Moreover, the finding contrasts with people's actual experiences of devolution in key public policy areas, something that is illustrated in the next section.

The Life and Times survey included a Northern Ireland version of the 'West Lothian question',[2] which sought to ascertain the extent to which respondents were satisfied with arrangements for the governance of Northern Ireland within the context of a devolved United Kingdom. Respondents were asked if Northern Ireland's members of the Westminster Parliament should be allowed to vote on matters pertaining only to England given the existence of the Northern Ireland Assembly (Table 7.5). Overall, responses to the question are inconclusive, with 35 per cent agreeing that Northern Ireland's Westminster MPs should be stripped of voting rights on exclusively English matters. While 28 per cent

Table 7.5 Northern Ireland MPs should no longer be allowed to
vote in the House of Commons on laws that only affect England (%)

	Protestant	Catholic	All
Agree strongly	7	7	7
Agree	22	37	28
Neither agree nor disagree	24	18	21
Disagree	24	16	20
Disagree strongly	11	5	8
Don't know	14	17	17

disagree with the proposition, 21 per cent neither agree nor disagree, and
a relatively high 17 per cent don't know.

A significant sectarian differential exists on this question, with 44 per cent
of Catholics agreeing with the statement that Northern Ireland's MPs
should not have voting rights over English matters, as against 29 per cent
of Protestants. The higher Protestant support for full participation in
Westminster may be based on a view that the Union depends on the total-
ity and interdependence of all of its political units. To give up full participation in Westminster matters may represent an erosion of Northern
Ireland's place within the Union. Equally, for nationalists, a stronger profession of disinterest in English matters has an ideological rationality; if
the basis of Irish nationalism is to minimise British influence over Irish
affairs, then Irish nationalists can have no intrinsic interest in the affairs of
another 'nation'. The higher figure for Catholics also suggests a greater
satisfaction with the Assembly (reflected elsewhere in the survey). For
many Protestants, maintaining full links with Westminster may be a recognition that ultimate sovereignty resides in Westminster and it is there that
guarantees of the Union can be best defended.

On whether the Northern Ireland Assembly was giving people in
Northern Ireland more or less say on how Northern Ireland was being
governed, 40 per cent of respondents say more, 8 per cent say less, and
44 per cent say that it was making no difference (Table 7.6). A 20 percentage point difference exists between the proportions of Catholics and
Protestants who say that the Assembly was giving people more say. In
other words, substantially more Catholics than Protestants felt empowered
by the Assembly. Interestingly, this does not translate into a widespread
Protestant feeling of disempowerment; only 12 per cent of Protestants feel
that the Assembly was giving people less say. Instead, Protestants tend to
hold a reserved rather than a negative judgement, with 50 per cent saying
that the Assembly was 'making no difference'.

Certainly the Assembly and Executive invested considerable energy
into consultation with key public and professional sectors and with
the wider population as well. Consultations on hospital services and

Table 7.6 Effect of the Assembly on ordinary people's say in how the region is governed (%)

	Protestant	Catholic	All
More say	31	51	40
Less say	12	3	8
Making no difference	50	39	44
Don't know	7	7	8

post-primary school education in particular received considerable media and public attention. Perhaps the relatively high figure of 40 per cent who feel that the Assembly was giving people greater say was a reflection of a type of governance that stood in marked contrast to direct rule in which decisions were made by civil servants in London and Belfast and, in some cases, moderated by unelected local committees of the great and the good, or QUANGOs.

ATTITUDES TOWARDS ASSEMBLY PERFORMANCE

While the survey findings reveal considerable public faith in the Assembly, perceptions of the Assembly's handling of key public policy areas such as health, education and the economy are mixed. It is worth noting that previous Life and Times surveys have recorded a consistent public wish for the prioritisation of health and education in day-to-day government activity, with health care having precedence. Indeed this prioritisation of health is reflected in other surveys across the United Kingdom (Taylor-Gooby and Hastie, 2002).

According to the 2001 Life and Times survey, perceptions of how health care was handled post-devolution reflect a sense of public disappointment. Comparison with the survey in 2000 shows a distinct public view that health care was getting worse under the Assembly. In 2000, 28 per cent of respondents said that health care was getting worse; by 2001 this figure had increased to 39 per cent (Table 7.7). Only 9 per cent in 2000 and 11 per cent in 2001 thought that health care was improving. Protestants are more inclined than Catholics to hold negative perceptions of health care under the Assembly. There may have been a 'Sinn Féin factor' in operation in explaining the negative opinion on health care. The Health, Social Services and Public Safety portfolio was held by Bairbre de Brún, a prominent member of Sinn Féin. Many unionists regarded Sinn Féin as unreconstructed terrorists and felt that their inclusion in the powersharing government amounted to the negation of democracy. The irony that a Sinn Féin minister was in charge of the health portfolio while the party's more militant siblings in the IRA were responsible for a significant drain on the health budget was lost on few unionists.

Table 7.7   Change in health care under the Assembly (%)

	2000	2001	2000	2001	2000	2001
	Protestant		Catholic		All	
Better	5	8	17	15	9	11
Worse	33	49	17	28	28	39
Same	51	30	59	42	52	35
Don't know/						
Too early to say	11	12	8	15	10	15

Table 7.8   Change in health care under the Assembly, by how respondents would vote if a fresh referendum were held on the Good Friday Agreement (%)

	Would vote yes	*Would vote no*
Better	14	8
Worse	31	58
Same	40	27
Too early to say	12	5
Don't know	3	1

However, the existence of a Sinn Féin factor among Protestants is only a partial explanation of the generally negative opinion on health care under devolution. Protestant faith in the health system suffered a sharp deterioration in the 2000 to 2001 period, under the tenure of the same minister. The proportion of Protestants who felt that health care deteriorated under the Assembly's steerage jumped by 16 percentage points between 2000 and 2001. Similarly, those who said that health care was the same as under the pre-devolution dispensation declined by 17 percentage points in the 2000 to 2001 period. Of those who said that they would vote 'no' in a fresh referendum on the Good Friday Agreement, an alarming 58 per cent say that health care became worse under the Assembly (Table 7.8). Only 14 per cent of putative 'yes' voters say that health care improved. Among Catholics the picture was also gloomy, with only 15 per cent believing that health care improved under devolution.

Health issues received considerable media attention during 2001; invariably it was negative attention such as the revelation that Northern Ireland had the highest waiting lists in the United Kingdom and the seeming indecision of the health minister in relation to acute hospital provision (BBC News Online, 26 June 2001; 26 December 2001). Since the survey was conducted, a number of announcements on major investment in the health sector have been made, and it will be interesting to see if subsequent surveys identify a dividend in terms of public perception (BBC News Online, 2 July 2002).

Perceptions of education under the Assembly are slightly more encouraging than those on health. A quarter of respondents (24 per cent) feel that education improved under the Assembly – double the 12 per cent who say that it became worse (Table 7.9). The largest proportion, 43 per cent, say it was the same as before, and 13 per cent believe that it is too early to say. Again sectarian differentials are noticeable, with twice as many Catholics as Protestants saying that education improved under the Assembly. Indeed, the proportion of Protestants who feel that education became worse under the Assembly almost doubled in the 2000 to 2001 period (from 10 to 19 per cent). Again a Sinn Féin factor may have been at work, with the prominent republican Martin McGuinness holding the portfolio. McGuinness had adopted an ambitious programme, which involved discarding school league tables and reforming post-primary education. The latter project attracted enormous attention, with newspapers, churches and political parties taking sides in an increasingly bitter debate. The debate adopted a sectarian character with the UUP and DUP strongly opposing proposals to change the powers of the post-primary sector to select pupils (Gallagher and Smith, 2002).

On the economy, Catholic reactions are more positive than those of Protestants (Table 7.10). Again the option that things 'remain the same as before' attracts most response.

On the question of whether the Northern Ireland Assembly represented good value for money, 35 per cent of respondents say that it definitely or probably did, as against 44 per cent who say that it definitely or probably

Table 7.9 Change in education under the Assembly (%)

	2000	2001	2000	2001	2000	2001
	Protestant		*Catholic*		*All*	
Better	9	15	32	37	16	24
Worse	10	19	1	5	8	12
Same	61	46	55	38	59	43
Don't know/						
Too early to say	20	20	13	20	18	21

Table 7.10 Change in the economy under the Assembly (%)

	Protestant	*Catholic*	*All*
Better	19	32	24
Worse	16	9	14
Same as before	44	41	42
Too early to say	11	13	12
Don't know	10	6	9

did not (Table 7.11). Over a half of Protestants (53 per cent) feel the
Assembly was poor value for money. Notably, a relatively high proportion
of respondents – 21 per cent – say that they don't know. Perhaps this suggests an issue of public presentation for the Assembly. Opinion on the
costs of devolution reflected that in Scotland and Wales where the spi-
ralling costs of architectural visions and administration made the headlines (*Guardian*, 2001; *Financial Times*, 2002).

In the period since the survey was carried out it was revealed that the
Office of the First Minister and the Deputy First Minister (OFMDFM)
employed more people than Downing Street and the Taoiseach's Office in
Dublin put together. In July 2002 OFMDFM employed 424 people. The
White House employs a little over 500.[3] This, and reports that
the Executive was underspending by up to £1 m per day, played poorly in
the local media and are unlikely to encourage the view that the Assembly
represents good value for money (BBC News Online, 28 June 2002). It is
worth remembering that while Northern Ireland's devolved institutions
may be blamed for how they choose to spend money, they have very little
control over how they raise funds (Heald and McLeod, 2002).

Despite this, the Life and Times survey in 1999 revealed that people
were prepared to consider tax increases to fund better public services.
Some 90 per cent of people said they would pay more income tax to fund
the health service. In 2000, the survey found support for the Assembly to
have its own tax-raising powers similar to those held by the Scottish
Parliament. Majorities of both Catholics (68 per cent) and Protestants
(52 per cent) supported the proposition (Table 7.12).

Table 7.11 Is the Assembly good value for money? (%)

	Protestant	Catholic	All
Yes, definitely	5	9	6
Yes, probably	23	35	29
No, probably not	29	25	26
No, definitely not	24	11	18
Don't know	19	20	21

Table 7.12 Should the Assembly have the power to raise
or lower income tax like the Scottish Parliament? (%)

	Protestant	Catholic	All
Yes	52	68	57
No	33	13	27
Don't know	15	18	16

Source: Life and Times 2000

Table 7.13   Do you think that the Assembly will still be in place in 3 years'
time? (%)

	2000	2001	2000	2001	2000	2001
	Protestant		Catholic		All	
Yes	41	52	65	69	50	58
No	27	19	9	8	21	14
Don't know	32	30	26	23	28	28

PERCEPTIONS OF THE FUTURE OF THE ASSEMBLY

Majorities in both communities – 52 per cent of Protestants and 69 per cent
of Catholics – believed that the Assembly would still be in place in three
years' time (Table 7.13). Moreover, when compared with the survey in 2000,
political optimism in both communities was rising, with Protestant opinion
on the permanence of the Assembly edging into a majority. The growing
optimism was misplaced however. On 14 October 2002, the Assembly was
suspended for a fourth time in its brief history. Allegations that the IRA had
a spy ring within the Northern Ireland Office (NIO) compounded persistent
unionist disquiet at continued IRA activity and the organisation's failure to
move beyond a partial decommissioning of its weapons stocks and counten-
ance disbandment. But the collapse of devolution had much deeper roots
and reflected the basic problem of attempting to accommodate mutually
exclusive nationalisms within the same political dispensation.

CONCLUSION

Given the political context, the findings from the Life and Times survey
produce a number of mildly encouraging responses. Public political discourse and the evident depth of enmity displayed between members of the
same government may have led to reasonable expectations of more
gloomy attitudes towards the Assembly. Instead, many survey respondents
show a willingness to give the devolution experiment a chance and suspend definitive judgements. But political circumstances, culminating in
the suspension of devolution in October 2002, meant that the experiment
was cut short. The patience displayed by many survey respondents is
unlikely to be infinite. The devolution experiment relied on the deferral of
constitutional and overtly political issues to give the devolved institutions
a chance to function. This has not happened and the context of devolution
became poisoned to the extent that the powersharing Executive collapsed.

Governments throughout industrial and post-industrial societies have
suffered from declining trust and legitimacy from the 1990s (Nye, 1997;
Putnam, 2000). Yet the findings of the 2001 Life and Times survey show

that traces of political optimism remain among respondents. There is a strong appetite for a greater devolution of powers and the majority feel that devolution was a model that would last for at least three years. The view that devolution was a threat to the Union is not widely shared. Four times as many survey respondents believed that a devolved Northern Ireland had a stronger voice in the United Kingdom than those who said it had a weaker voice. The relatively positive attitudes towards devolution were reflected by the widespread dismay among pro-Agreement parties and policy specialists that greeted the suspension of devolution in October 2002 (BBC News Online, 10 October 2002). One Ulster Unionist member of the Legislative Assembly noted that 'unfortunately the good solid work being done by many in the Assembly has been put on hold' and went on to warn against the unaccountability of direct rule (Beggs, 2002). Martin McGuinness pressed the incoming education minister to uphold his plans for a scrapping of the schools transfer test (BBC News Online, 17 October 2002). The former finance minister, Sean Farren, appealed that the Assembly's public policy plans be implemented by the direct rule ministers (*Irish News*, 2002a). One nursing professional despaired that the incoming NIO minister would only spend four hours a week on the health portfolio (*Irish News*, 2002b).

Yet the attachment to devolution, as portrayed in the survey results, and the dismay at the reintroduction of direct rule were not enough to save this form of government. Instead the demands of ethnic particularism held more sway than the perceived advantages of devolution. This ethnic particularism was especially wicked in that intergroup mistrust, most notably between Sinn Féin and unionists, was complemented by intragroup competition, most notably within unionism. Should devolution be resurrected, it will be interesting to see if the traces of political optimism will have survived the stay in cold storage. It will also be interesting to see if the devolved institutions have the capacity, as presently formulated, to deal with the distinct sectarian differential in their approval rating. It may be that only structural change, namely the exclusion of Sinn Féin, will be enough to assuage Protestant concerns. If this is the case, and if Sinn Féin remains the largest nationalist party, then self-government may be unsustainable.

NOTES

1. Cited in BBC News Online, 30 October 2001. Survey evidence on the desire for regional government in England is inconclusive. The 2001 British Social Attitudes survey found low levels of support for the establishment of regional assemblies in England. In the most pro-devolution areas, the north east and north west, less than a third of respondents favoured regional government. See Table 8.6 in Heath, Rothon and Jarvis (2002). A 2002

BBC survey found much higher levels of support, with the north east and north west both showing 72 per cent support for the regional assemblies. See Tomaney (2002).

2. The 'West Lothian question' was originally asked by Tam Dalywell, the Labour MP for that constituency. He asked if it was right that a Scottish Labour Westminster MP could vote on education issues affecting only English constituencies while English MPs would not have the same rights regarding education in Scotland if there was a devolved Scottish Parliament.

3. Wilson (2002b). The 'inflation' of the numbers employed by the First and Deputy First Ministers was subsequently disputed by Gudgin (2002).

REFERENCES

Beggs, R. Jr (2002) 'Direct rule is unaccountable', 22 October, Ulster Unionist Party website <http:// www. uup.org/current/displayfullpress.asp? pressid=537>.

Bell, C. (2001) *Peace Agreements and Human Rights* (Oxford: Oxford University Press).

BBC News Online (26 June 2001) 'NI health service's serial reviews' <http://news. bbc.co.uk/1/hi/northern_ireland/1408577.stm>.

BBC News Online (30 October 2001) 'PM praises devolution "clout" ' <http://news. bbc.co.uk/1/hi/wales/1628485.stm>.

BBC News Online (26 December 2001) 'Health services under pressure' <http://news. bbc.co.uk/1/hi/northern_ireland/1710610.stm>.

BBC News Online (28 June 2002) 'Underspend reports "disgraceful" ' <http://news. bbc.co.uk/1/hi/northern_ireland/2071327.stm>.

BBC News Online (2 July 2002) 'Cancer centre gets green light' <http://news.bbc. co.uk/1/hi/northern_ireland/2079757.stm>.

BBC News Online (10 October 2002) 'Dismay at plans to suspend Assembly' <http://news. bbc.co.uk/1/hi/northern_ireland/2317795.stm>.

BBC News Online (17 October 2002) 'McGuinness passes on education brief' <http://news. bbc.co.uk/1/hi/northern_ireland/2334485.stm>.

BBC News Online (2 December 2002) 'No popping corks for NI devolution' <http://news. bbc.co.uk/1/hi/northern_ireland/2535939.stm>.

Financial Times (2002) 'Devolution has more than doubled cost of administering government in Wales', 8 March.

Gallagher, T. and Smith, A. (2002) 'Attitudes to academic selection, integrated education and diversity within the curriculum' in A.M. Gray, K. Lloyd, P. Devine, G. Robinson and D. Heenan (eds) *Social Attitudes in Northern Ireland: The Eighth Report* (London: Pluto Press) pp.120–37.

Guardian (2001) '£200 m and rising, Scotland's "dome" takes shape', 23 June.

Gudgin, G. (2002) 'Counting heads at OFMDFM', *Fortnight*, Issue 408, November, p. 7.

Hansard (27 February 2001) Official Report of the Northern Ireland Assembly <http://www.ni-assembly.gov.uk/record/reports/010227.htm>.

Hansard (24 September 2001) Official Report of the Northern Ireland Assembly <http://www.ni-assembly.gov.uk/record/reports/010924.htm>.

Heald, D. and McLeod, A. (2002) 'Beyond Barnett? Financing devolution' in J. Adams and P. Robinson (eds) *Devolution in Practice: Public Policy Differences within the UK* (London: Institute of Public Policy Research) pp. 147–75.

Heath, A., Rothon, C. and Jarvis, L. (2002) 'English to the core?' in A. Park, J. Curtice, K. Thomson, L. Jarvis and C. Bromley (eds) *British Social Attitudes: The 19th Report* (London: Sage) pp. 169–84.

Irish News (2002a) 'Appeal to ministers to honour commitments', 11 December.

Irish News (2002b) 'Minister spends "four hours a week" on health', 5 November.

MacGinty, R. and Darby, J. (2002) *Guns and Government: The Management of the Northern Ireland Peace Process* (Houndmills: Palgrave).

Nye, J. (1997) 'In government we don't trust', *Foreign Policy*, Vol. 108, Fall, pp. 99–111.

Putnam, R. (2000) *Bowling Alone: The Collapse and Revival of American Community* (New York: Simon and Schuster).

Reid, J. (2001) 'Becoming persuaders – British and Irish identities in Northern Ireland', speech by the Secretary of State Dr John Reid MP to the Institute of Irish Studies, Liverpool University, 21 November.

Taylor-Gooby, P. and Hastie, C. (2002) 'Support for state spending: has New Labour got it right?' in A. Park, J. Curtice, K. Thomson, L. Jarvis and C. Bromley (eds) *British Social Attitudes: The 19th Report* (London: Sage) pp. 75–96.

Tomaney, J. (2002) 'The evolution of English regionalism', *Regional Studies*, Vol. 36, No. 7, pp. 722–31.

Wilford, R. (2001a) 'The Assembly' in *Devolution Monitoring Programme Northern Ireland*, Report 9, November (Belfast: Democratic Dialogue) <http://www.democratic dialogue.org/devolution.htm>.

Wilford, R. (ed.) (2001b) *Aspects of the Belfast Agreement* (Oxford: Oxford University Press).

Wilford, R. (2002) 'The Assembly' in *Devolution Monitoring Programme Northern Ireland*, Report 10, February (Belfast: Democratic Dialogue) <http://www.democratic dialogue.org/devolution.htm>.

Wilson, R. (2002a) 'Devolved government' in *Devolution Monitoring Programme Northern Ireland*, Report 10, February (Belfast: Democratic Dialogue) <http://www.democratic dialogue.org/devolution.htm>.

Wilson, R. (2002b), 'Devolved government' in *Devolution Monitoring Programme Northern Ireland*, Report 12, August (Belfast: Democratic Dialogue) <http://www.democratic dialogue.org/devolution.htm>.

8

The Impact of Devolution on Community Relations

Jeremy Harbison and Anna Manwah Lo

The eighth report on social attitudes in Northern Ireland (Gray, Lloyd, Devine, Robinson and Heenan, 2002) included a chapter by Hughes and Donnelly reviewing ten years of social attitudes to community relations in Northern Ireland from 1989 to 1999. Data came from the Northern Ireland Social Attitudes surveys (1989 to 1996) and the Northern Ireland Life and Times surveys (1998 and 1999). Fieldwork for the 1999 Northern Ireland Life and Times survey took place between October 1999 and mid-January 2000, which coincided with the devolution of power from Westminster to the locally elected Assembly in December 1999. The current chapter considers whether experience of devolution over the succeeding two years has demonstrated any impact on the fraught area of relationships between communities in Northern Ireland.

Hughes and Donnelly (2002) noted that evidence from the 1999 Life and Times survey indicated that while there was a general improvement in attitudes towards community relations over the ten-year period from 1989 to 1999, the Catholic and Protestant communities appeared to have developed notably different attitudes on a range of issues. Catholics in general appeared more positive towards efforts to promote cross-community contact and were more confident that their rights and cultural traditions would be protected. Protestants, in contrast, appeared less keen on mixing, less confident in their identity and in their belief that cultural traditions would be protected.

The time period covered in this chapter encompasses two years of critical development in society in Northern Ireland. The region has experienced, albeit somewhat spasmodically, the outworking of the Good Friday Agreement through the establishment of an inclusive four-party Executive and the transfer of power to a locally-elected Assembly. A number of important political advances occurred during this period. The Executive of the Assembly agreed both a Programme for Government for Northern Ireland and a supporting budget. In this Programme for Government the four parties in the Executive committed themselves to working towards a future in which Northern Ireland became

> a peaceful, cohesive, inclusive, prosperous, stable and fair society, firmly founded on the achievement of reconciliation, tolerance and mutual trust and the protection and vindication of the human rights of all. This vision is one based on partnership, equality and mutual respect as the basis of relationships within Northern Ireland, between North and South and between these islands. (Northern Ireland Executive, 2001)

In the Programme for Government, the Executive recognised the importance of promoting better relationships within the community in the achievement of this future. One of the key actions identified was to review and put in place a cross-departmental strategy for the promotion of community relations. The Executive saw this strategy as necessary to produce a significant improvement in community relations, and believed that it would reduce the causes of conflict between communities, especially at the physical interfaces (Office of the First Minister and Deputy First Minister (OFMDFM), 2001). The draft strategy had not been produced at the point of suspension of the Assembly in the autumn of 2002.

Other significant political achievements during this two-year period included the establishment of a cross-community Policing Board involving political representation from the Ulster Unionist Party (UUP), the Democratic Unionist Party (DUP) and the Social Democratic and Labour Party (SDLP) – but not Sinn Féin – to oversee the new Police Service for Northern Ireland. Regionally distinct social and economic priorities were identified through the Programme for Government, for example free travel for the elderly. Continuing economic progress was demonstrated, with increasing numbers in employment and significant falls in numbers and levels of unemployment. In the Assembly, the committee system developed generally effectively, with members from the range of political parties cooperating and bringing significantly greater accountability through the operation of government departments, for example through the work of the Public Accounts Committee. The ability of a local minister to sensitively and competently handle crises, such as the foot and mouth epidemic, was apparent.

Against this progress, the two-year period saw darker developments. The unionist position to engaging in an Executive with Sinn Féin caused continuing tensions both between the two main unionist parties and within the UUP. The establishment of the new Police Service was associated with the demise of the Royal Ulster Constabulary (RUC). This issue, along with the release of large numbers of IRA prisoners, provoked increasing unionist concern. There was, alongside the growing fragmentation of unionist political opinion, a violent feud between the two main loyalist paramilitary groups, the Ulster Defence Association and the Ulster Volunteer Force. Elections in the period saw a significant move in support within both main communities towards the more extreme parties from the more moderate. On the ground, sectarian confrontation increased, most notably in north Belfast, leading to demands for greater physical intervention to separate the two communities. Punishment beatings and shootings increased, and police figures showed that 2001 had been the most violent year since the paramilitary ceasefires of 1994 (Police Service of Northern Ireland, 2002).

The Life and Times surveys completed in 2000 and 2001 have therefore paralleled a major effort at transforming the nature of Northern Ireland society. A devolved Assembly and Executive were established and operated for much of the two years, with a cross-party commitment to develop a more inclusive, tolerant and cohesive society. Against the progress made by and through such political developments, there continued a backdrop of sectarian violence, paramilitary action both within and between communities, and continuing-internal political dissension, especially within the unionist family.

This chapter explores three areas: firstly, it extends the Hughes and Donnelly (2002) analysis from a ten- to a twelve-year period and considers whether the trends identified have continued, or whether the experience of devolution has indeed led to a more cohesive and integrated society; secondly, it considers in greater detail changes over the key two-year period 1999 to 2001; and thirdly, in response to the aspiration for Northern Ireland to become a more tolerant and cohesive society, attitudes to minority ethnic groups are considered. The importance and extent of racial prejudice in Northern Ireland has increasingly been recognised, and the need for good relationships to include all groupings, racial as well as religious, has been a recent legislative and policy issue.

SOCIAL ATTITUDES FROM 1989 TO 2001

This section considers data derived from the Northern Ireland Social Attitudes surveys from 1989 to 1996 and from Life and Times survey material from 1998 onwards. A number of questions was asked throughout these series, which were identical or virtually identical and which enabled an assessment of trends in attitudes to be monitored. The figures for 'all respondents' include those who say they have no religion or are of another religion.

Relations between Protestants and Catholics

Respondents were asked whether relations between Protestants and Catholics were better, worse or the same as they were five years ago. Table 8.1 shows the results for those who believed relations were better than five years ago. Perceived relations between Protestants and Catholics significantly improved from 1989 until the mid-1990s; since then, however, respondents appear considerably more pessimistic, and by the end of 2001, both Protestants and Catholics were reporting attitudes close to those first assessed in 1989.

In particular, in the period of greatest interest to this chapter covering the years 2000 and 2001, there is evidence of a serious downturn in views about relationships between the two communities.

When respondents were asked whether they believed that in five years' time the situation would be better than now, similar changes in attitudes can be detected. Table 8.2 shows the percentage of respondents who believe that relations will be better in the future. By 1995, almost two-thirds of those interviewed were generally optimistic in their future expectations, although Catholics were considerably more positive (78 per cent) than Protestants (52 per cent). However, expectations have changed markedly since then, particularly over the last two years of the series. The more pessimistic perceptions are evident among both Protestant and Catholic respondents, although Catholics remain consistently more positive than Protestants.

Sharing in housing, employment and education

Throughout the twelve years of the survey period, attempts have been made regularly to assess the attitudes of people in Northern Ireland

Table 8.1 Are relations between Protestants and Catholics better now than 5 years ago? (% saying yes)

	1989	1991	1993	1994	1995	1996	1998	1999	2000	2001
Protestants	20	29	25	26	51	43	44	42	37	25
Catholics	23	31	27	26	62	47	60	60	52	33
All	22	29	25	26	56	45	50	50	42	28

Table 8.2 Will relations between Protestants and Catholics be better in 5 years' time? (% saying yes)

	1989	1991	1993	1994	1995	1996	1998	1999	2000	2001
Protestants	22	30	27	30	52	39	53	46	37	27
Catholics	30	40	32	36	78	48	75	67	48	40
All	26	34	29	32	63	43	62	55	40	33

towards mixing or sharing in where they live, work or where they would send their children to school. One question asked of respondents was, if they had a choice, whether they would prefer to live in a neighbourhood with people of only their own religion or in a mixed-religion neighbour-hood. Table 8.3 shows the percentage saying that they would prefer to live in a mixed-religion neighbourhood. A willingness for greater integrated living peaked at 83 per cent in 1996, followed by a progressive decline in those indicating such a preference until, by 2001, overall 66 per cent indi-cated such a preference. While Catholics consistently report stronger pref-erences for living in mixed-religion areas, by 2001 lower percentages of both Protestants and Catholics are suggesting such a preference compared with the start of the survey period in 1989.

Similar changes in attitude towards working in mixed-religion work-places can be seen in Table 8.4. By 1996, 95 per cent of all respondents said they would prefer to work in a mixed-religion workplace. There is progressive decay from this position, particularly across the years 2000 and 2001, and by the end of the time period in question, fewer people from both Protestant and Catholic communities are indicating a preference to work in a mixed-religion workplace than was the position in 1989.

Education is seen by many as central to the development of more posi-tive relationships within Northern Ireland (O Connor, 2002). The surveys asked respondents if they were deciding where to send their children to school, would they prefer a school with children of only their own religion or a mixed-religion school.

Less variability in attitude can be detected, with around 50 to 60 per cent of all respondents indicating that they would prefer to send their

Table 8.3 Would you prefer to live in a mixed-religion neighbourhood? (% saying yes)

	1989	1991	1993	1995	1996	1998	1999	2000	2001
Protestants	67	64	67	73	81	66	68	67	59
Catholics	75	76	82	83	85	74	79	73	72
All	71	70	74	78	83	71	73	70	66

Table 8.4 Would you prefer to work in a mixed-religion workplace? (% saying yes)

	1989	1991	1993	1995	1996	1998	1999	2000	2001
Protestants	82	85	87	89	95	78	82	80	70
Catholics	86	88	94	93	97	85	91	83	82
All	84	87	90	91	95	82	86	81	76

children to a mixed-religion school across the twelve years (Table 8.5). It is worth noting, however, that only around 5 per cent of children of school age actually attended such mixed-religion schools in 2001 (Department of Education, 2002).

Constitutional issues

Finally, in this section, attitudes towards constitutional issues relating to Northern Ireland are considered. Over the years of the surveys, respondents have been asked whether the long-term policy for Northern Ireland should be for it to remain part of the United Kingdom or to become part of a unified Ireland, and whether a united Ireland is likely within the next 20 years.

Table 8.6 shows a steady erosion in the percentage of respondents who see the best long-term policy as remaining part of the United Kingdom. Of particular interest is the decline in the percentage of Protestants who see this as the best solution, from 93 per cent in 1989 to 79 per cent by 2001. There is a similar decline in the much smaller proportion of Catholics who see this as the best solution. Predictably there are clear differences between the main communities in their response to this question. It is noticeable that in 2001 there is some evidence of an increase in the percentage of Catholics who see a reunited Ireland as the preferred solution, again to a level higher than in 1989.

Despite the continuing and strikingly different attitudes towards the best long-term policy for Northern Ireland between the two main communities, there is greater agreement between them in seeing whether a united Ireland is very or quite unlikely in the next 20 years (Table 8.7). In 1989, 65 per cent of all respondents thought this would be the case, but this proportion fell to

Table 8.5   Would you prefer to send your children to a mixed-religion school? (% saying yes)

	1989	1991	1993	1995	1996	1998	1999	2000	2001
Protestants	52	51	53	59	67	54	57	55	55
Catholics	54	49	52	56	57	52	72	52	63
All	55	52	56	61	65	56	66	55	60

Table 8.6   What should the long-term policy for Northern Ireland be? (%)

	1989	1993	1995	1999	2001
Remain part of UK					
Protestant	93	89	86	87	79
Catholic	32	36	34	16	15
Reunify with rest of Ireland					
Protestant	3	6	7	3	5
Catholic	56	49	56	48	59

38 per cent by 2001. In 2001, only 39 per cent of Protestants see such an outcome in the next 20 years as very or quite unlikely.

DETAILED ATTITUDINAL CHANGES

The previous section reported data on the extended time series of survey information from 1989 to 2001. The data suggest a continuing deterioration in attitudes towards community relationships in general, though somewhat different profiles for Catholics and Protestants appear, with Protestants generally more negative. This section considers some responses from the 2001 survey in greater detail to try and further illuminate the changing position.

Table 8.8 shows the percentages of respondents who agree or strongly agree that their cultural tradition is always the underdog in Northern Ireland. There has been a striking increase among Protestants who feel this, with 37 per cent in 2001 – more than double the 1998 figure. Catholic views are generally fairly constant over the period.

The differences between the two communities are striking. Table 8.9 shows the percentage who agree and those who disagree that their own

Table 8.7 A united Ireland in the next 20 years is 'very unlikely' or 'quite unlikely' (%)

	1989	1993	1995	1999	2001
Protestants	64	68	48	49	39
Catholics	65	71	59	40	38
All	65	69	53	45	38

Table 8.8 Respondents who 'agree' or 'strongly agree' that their cultural tradition is always the underdog (%)

	1998	1999	2000	2001
Protestants	17	19	22	37
Catholics	31	34	24	28
All	22	24	21	32

Table 8.9 Respondents who 'agree' or 'disagree' that they are confident their cultural tradition is protected (%)

	Agree	Disagree
Protestants	30	39
Catholics	70	9
All	48	24

cultural tradition is protected in Northern Ireland. While only 30 per cent of Protestants agree with this statement, 70 per cent of Catholics believe that their cultural tradition is protected. In contrast, 39 per cent of Protestants disagree compared with only 9 per cent of Catholics.

A number of questions in the survey examined views towards the Peace Process. Again, very contrasting views are held by Protestants and Catholics. Table 8.10 summarises the views of respondents about the search for peace over the last few years. Just over a half of Catholics are happy, which is twice the percentage of Protestants who feel the same (54 per cent and 26 per cent respectively), while significantly larger proportions of Protestants than Catholics are unhappy, disappointed, angry or feel betrayed about the process.

Similar differences are reflected when people were asked how they personally feel about what might happen over the next few years. Again more than double the percentage of Catholics are optimistic or confident than Protestants (Table 8.11) and 20 per cent of Protestants indicate they are worried about the future compared with 6 per cent of Catholics.

There has been concern that the intensive drive on equality through legislation and associated action (such as the requirement to develop Equality Schemes by public bodies or the formal monitoring requirements based on religious affiliation) could lead to a deterioration in relationships as equality, especially in employment terms, was perceived as a 'zero sum game' between the communities. Results do not indicate that people of either main community see themselves as individually discriminated against in the workplace (Table 8.12). Very small proportions believe that they have been refused a job, treated unfairly in promotion or treated unfairly by their

Table 8.10   Feelings about the search for peace (%)

	Happy	Mixed	Disappointed	Unhappy	Betrayed	Angry
Protestants	26	45	20	6	14	8
Catholics	54	36	12	4	2	4
All	39	41	16	5	8	6

Note: Respondents could give more than one answer

Table 8.11   Feelings about the search for peace in the future (%)

	Optimistic	Confident	Mixed	Worried
Protestants	22	10	45	20
Catholics	45	21	25	6
All	33	15	34	14

colleagues because of their religion over the last ten years. Equally impor-
tantly, when people were asked whether there was a continuing need for
equality laws in Northern Ireland, only 19 per cent of Protestants and 11 per
cent of Catholics agreed that there was no need for such legislation.

Results considered to date have suggested that while there has been a
deterioration generally in cross-community relationships this has been
especially evident among Protestants. In an attempt to examine some of
the underlying factors associated with these changes, a more detailed consideration of Protestant attitudes in terms of differing age or educational
level was undertaken. These results are summarised in Table 8.13.

The table shows that, consistently, respondents with lower levels of
educational qualifications are more pessimistic about relationships

Table 8.12 Aspects of equality: respondents who ... (%)

	Protestants	Catholics
Have been refused a job because of their religion in the last 10 years	3	4
Have been treated unfairly in promotion because of their religion in the last 10 years	3	3
Have been treated unfairly by their colleagues because of their religion in the last 10 years	3	4
Believe there is no need for equality laws in Northern Ireland	19	11

Table 8.13 Attitudes, age and educational level of Protestant respondents (%)

	Educational level		Age	
	A level or higher	Less than A level	40 and under	41+
Relations between Protestants and Catholics are worse than 5 years ago	14	23	20	23
Relations between Protestants and Catholics will be worse in 5 years' time	10	16	18	13
Agree/strongly agree that their cultural tradition is always the underdog	15	21	19	18
Worried about what might happen in search for peace	16	19	22	19
Happy about search for peace over last 5 years	29	24	19	30
Prefer to live in neighbourhood with people of only own religion	21	38	38	30
Prefer a workplace with people of only own religion	12	25	22	20
Prefer a school with children of only own religion	25	43	40	36

between Catholics and Protestants both currently and in the future, believe that their cultural tradition is always the underdog, worry more about the peace process over the next five years, are less happy that progress has been made, and very clearly show a preference to live, work and send their children to schools with members of their own religious group. There appears to be some difference by age group, in that younger Protestants (aged 40 years or under) appear more negative in their views.

BROADER COMMUNITY RELATIONSHIPS

Until recently, consideration of relationships between communities in Northern Ireland has been dominated by the tensions between the two main religious groupings. Increasingly, however, there has been appreciation that issues relating to life experiences of minority ethnic groups warrant consideration and that racial prejudice is a significant problem in the community (Connolly and Keenan, 2000).

Such growing appreciation has been reflected by the introduction of the Race Relations (Northern Ireland) Order 1997, which makes racial discrimination unlawful. The Northern Ireland Act 1998 further recognised the issue by requiring all public authorities to develop Equality Schemes demonstrating how they intend to promote equality of opportunity and good relations between persons of different racial groups (as well as between other identified groups).

The 2001 survey explored attitudes to some minority ethnic groups in Northern Ireland. The Northern Ireland Social Attitudes survey in 1994 and the 1998 Life and Times survey also included some similar questions allowing some comparisons over time to be made.

Table 8.14 indicates the percentage of respondents who think that minority ethnic groups are treated better, worse or the same as five years ago compared with the situation found in 1994. There is little difference between the two years, with the majority of people in both years believing that minority ethnic groups are generally treated the same as they were five years before.

Table 8.14 How are minority ethnic groups generally treated compared with 5 years ago? (%)

	1994	2001
Better	19	19
Worse	12	7
Same	63	52
Don't know	6	22

A number of questions explored the extent to which respondents would willingly accept and mix with members of minority ethnic groups. Table 8.15 records the percentage saying whether they themselves would mind 'a lot' or 'a little' if a suitably qualified person of Chinese origin were appointed as their boss, and the proportion who would mind if a close relative were to marry a person of Chinese origin. Figures for the years 1994, 1998 and 2001 suggest some increase in those who would mind having a boss of Chinese origin (from 11 per cent in 1994 to 19 per cent in 2001), but little change in attitudes towards a close relative marrying a person of Chinese origin. Across all years, around one-third of respondents say they would mind a little or a lot.

On the basis that individuals may be reluctant to admit to such personal prejudice, additional questions asked respondents whether they thought that 'most people' would mind if a suitably qualified person of Chinese origin were appointed as their boss or if a close relative were to marry a person of Chinese origin. Table 8.16 shows the percentages of respondents

Table 8.15 Respondents indicating they personally would mind 'a little' or 'a lot' if ... (%)

	1994	1998	2001
A suitably qualified person of Chinese origin were appointed their boss	11	15	19
A suitably qualified person of a different religion were appointed their boss	*	8	12
A close relative were to marry a person of Chinese origin	32	31	31
A close relative were to marry a person of a different religion	*	26	28

* This question was not asked in 1994

Table 8.16 Respondents indicating most people would mind 'a little' or 'a lot' if ... (%)

	1994	1998	2001
A suitably qualified person of Chinese origin were appointed their boss	34	34	39
A suitably qualified person of a different religion were appointed their boss	*	29	27
A close relative were to marry a person of Chinese origin	55	52	48
A close relative were to marry a person of a different religion	*	51	54

* This question was not asked in 1994

who believed that most people would mind a lot or a little for the three separate years. It indicates little change over the period 1994 to 2001, with high levels of negativity across the time period; the figures also tend to confirm that many people, while not choosing to voice their own negative feelings, are willing to attribute them to others.

Just over one-third of all respondents believe that most people would mind a lot or a little if a suitably qualified person of Chinese origin were appointed as their boss, and around a half believe that most people would have concern if a close relative were to marry a person of Chinese origin.

Tables 8.15 and 8.16 also include information on attitudes relating to having a boss of a different religion, or to a close relative marrying a person of a different religion. Table 8.15 shows that the level of negative attitudes towards a close relative marrying someone of a different religion is similar to those for a close relative marrying someone of Chinese origin. Table 8.16 shows a similar pattern when respondents are asked about the attitudes of 'most people'. There is considerable difference, however, in respondents' perception of whether 'most people' would mind a lot or a little if their boss were of Chinese origin or of a different religion. More respondents show negative attitudes towards having a boss of Chinese origin than having a boss from a different religion.

The 2001 survey also explored whether respondents thought that a range of specified groups are generally treated unfairly; 23 per cent of respondents believe that disabled persons are treated unfairly, and a similar proportion (22 per cent) believes that Travellers are treated unfairly. Smaller proportions feel that other minority ethnic groups, Protestants and Catholics are treated unfairly (10, 11 and 8 per cent respectively).

CONCLUSION

The introduction to this chapter reviewed political developments since 1999 – the end of the time period considered by Hughes and Donnelly (2002). This overlapped with the first experience in Northern Ireland of devolved government for 30 years. A number of major political developments associated with the outworking of the Good Friday Agreement, which aspired to produce a more stable and integrated society, had taken place. However, the period was also associated with evidence of increased polarisation between and within the communities, higher levels of sectarian and paramilitary violence and a deepening concern, particularly among Protestants, as to the political future. The survey results reported in this chapter are a worrying parallel to the political developments.

Overall, community attitudes have fallen from the most optimistic period of the mid-1990s to a position similar to, or worse than, those reflected in the 1989 survey. Both main communities demonstrate a deterioration in intercommunity attitudes, but there is increasing evidence that Protestants feel that there is a growing threat to their political and cultural identity. In general, Catholics remain more positive and optimistic about current and future relationships, and exhibit a greater willingness to integrate.

The negative views about community relationships, increased sharing and integration appear to be held more strongly by younger, and by less well-educated, members of the Protestant community. Further, there is little evidence that the implementation of the 1997 Race Relations (Northern Ireland) Order or actions to promote better relationships between persons of different racial groups are having any significant impact on the extent of negative racial attitudes expressed in Northern Ireland.

The results emphasise the critical importance for government in Northern Ireland to initiate urgent, broadly based and strategic action to achieve the Executive's vision as set out in the Programme for Government. The survey evidence, supported by other data on increasing and continuing physical segregation across such key areas as housing, schooling and the delivery of many other major public services (for example, Cairns and Darby, 1998) leads to a fundamental question about the future nature of Northern Ireland society. Should there be an acceptance of these ongoing trends towards a more segregated society, where action would be to attempt to stabilise relationships within and between the two main communities, or should policy encourage and promote a more integrated and shared society at every level? If the latter option is clearly and unambiguously identified as the preferred policy aim, government must set out clear policy objectives and, working with all key stakeholders and sectors in society, put in place an integrated and overarching strategic plan to promote better relationships within and between communities and groups in Northern Ireland. The current position would appear increasingly untenable, and there is an urgent need for political leadership to articulate the clear, unambiguous and specific vision for the nature of society to which all in Northern Ireland should commit.

REFERENCES

Cairns, E. and Darby, J. (1998) 'The conflict in Northern Ireland': reasons, consequences and controls, *American Psychologist*, Vol. 53, No. 7, pp. 754–60.

Connolly, P. and Keenan, M. (2000) *Racial Attitudes and Prejudice in Northern Ireland* (Belfast: Northern Ireland Statistics and Research Agency).

Department of Education (2002) *Enrolments at Schools and in Funded Pre-school Education in Northern Ireland 2001/2002* (Bangor: Statistics Branch Press Release).

Gray, A.M., Lloyd, K., Devine, P., Robinson, G. and Heenan, D. (eds) (2002) *Social Attitudes in Northern Ireland: The Eighth Report* (London: Pluto Press).

Hughes, J. and Donnelly, C. (2002) 'Ten years of social attitudes in Northern Ireland' in A.M. Gray, K. Lloyd, P. Devine, G. Robinson and D. Heenan (eds) *Social Attitudes in Northern Ireland: The Eighth Report* (London: Pluto Press) pp. 39–55.

Northern Ireland Executive (2001) *Making a Difference: The Programme for Government* (Belfast: Office of the First Minister and Deputy First Minister).

O Connor, F. (2002) *A Shared Childhood: The Story of Integrated Schools in Northern Ireland* (Belfast: Northern Ireland Council for Integrated Education).

Office of the First Minister and Deputy First Minister (2001) *Mallon Announces Review of Community Relations Policy* (Belfast: Executive Information Service) 30 April.

Police Service of Northern Ireland (2002) *Chief Constable's Annual Report 2001–2002* (Belfast: Police Service of Northern Ireland).

Appendix I
Technical Details of the Survey

Paula Devine

The chapters within this book primarily use data from the 2000 and 2001 Life and Times surveys. However, some chapters also refer to data from the 1998 and 1999 Life and Times surveys (Gray, Lloyd, Devine, Robinson and Heenan, 2002), as well as from the Northern Ireland Social Attitudes Survey series which ran from 1989 to 1996 (Stringer and Robinson, 1991, 1992, 1993; Breen, Devine and Robinson, 1995; Breen, Devine and Dowds, 1996; Dowds, Devine and Breen, 1997; Robinson, Heenan, Gray and Thompson, 1998). For comparative purposes, reference is also made to other attitudes surveys, such as the British Social Attitudes survey.

THE OVERALL DESIGN

The Life and Times survey involves face-to-face interviews with adults aged 18 years and over. The main part of the interview is carried out using computer-assisted personal interviewing (CAPI) and the respondent is also asked to complete a self-completion questionnaire. In 2000, there were two versions of the self-completion questionnaire, while there was only one version in 2001.

SURVEY CONTENT

The survey consists of a set of modules, which varies between years, although most modules are designed to be carried out on a regular basis, so that time-series data can be collected in years to come. However, two modules – Political Attitudes and Community Relations – are undertaken annually.

Not all modules are asked of the full adult sample. Where a smaller sample size is sufficient for a module, the sample is 'split', such that only a half of respondents is asked those questions. For example, the structure of the 2001 survey allowed for half the sample to be asked the questions within the Health Issues module, while the other half were asked questions within the Culture, Arts and Leisure module. The modules included in the 2000 and 2001 surveys are shown in Table A1.1.

The questions asked as part of the International Social Survey Programme (ISSP) are included in the self-completion questionnaires. In 2000 this module focused on Environment, and on Social Networks in 2001.

SAMPLING METHODOLOGY

The Postcode Address File (PAF) is used as the survey sampling frame, and is a comprehensive database of addresses in Northern Ireland. The sampling process begins by stratifying Northern Ireland into three geographic regions – Belfast, east of the Bann and west of the Bann – based on an amalgamation of District Council Areas. This stratification is undertaken

Table A1.1   Survey content by year

	Version A	Version B
2000	Background	Background
	Men's Life and Times	Men's Life and Times
	Community Relations	Community Relations
	Political Attitudes	Political Attitudes
	Welfare Reform	Welfare Reform
	Environment (ISSP)	Work Orientations
2001	Background	Background
	Education	Education
	Political Attitudes	Political Attitudes
	Health Issues	Culture, Arts and Leisure
	Community Relations	Community Relations
	Social Networks (ISSP)	Social Networks (ISSP)

to ensure that areas of lower population density, such as those west of the Bann, are adequately represented, and is standard practice in Northern Ireland social surveys. A random sample of addresses is then taken from each stratum, with probability proportionate to the number of addresses within it.

The next stage involves randomly selecting one adult to be interviewed from each household, which is achieved by the interviewer carrying out a Kish grid procedure. In this way, one adult is randomly selected from a household, which itself is randomly selected. However, this introduces a bias, as an adult living in a household with a large number of adults is less likely to be asked to take part than adults living in small or single adult households. To compensate for this, the data are weighted by a weight factor (WTFACTOR), which is based on the number of adults within the household. During the interview with the selected adult, information is collected on the age and gender of every member of the household, as well as their relationship to the respondent.

FIELDWORK

Households identified in the sample were sent an advance letter, which explained the purpose of the survey, outlined the method by which an individual respondent would be selected from the household, and requested cooperation with the project. The letter provided households with contact details for the project team and the fieldwork company, and also confirmed that a donation of £1 would be made to Action Cancer on behalf of each respondent.

For each year of the survey, fieldwork took place during October to December. Interviewing was carried out by social survey interviewers employed by Research and Evaluation Services (RES). Every fieldworker attended a briefing session conducted jointly by RES and members of the Life and Times survey team.

All interviews were conducted in the respondents' homes. Interviewers made up to a maximum of five calls before the person identified in the sample was deemed to be non-obtainable. Table A1.2 shows the status of addresses, and the number of addresses identified as 'in scope'. The self-completion form was either completed and handed back to the interviewer at the time of the main interview, or the interviewer called back at a later stage to collect it.

Table A1.2 Status of addresses

Year	Addresses issued	Vacant/Derelict/ Commercial	Total in scope
2000	2,850	42	2,808
2001	2,820	145	2,675

Table A1.3 Breakdown of response

	2000		2001	
	Number	%	Number	%
Achieved	1,800	64	1,800	67
Refused	428	15	482	18
Non-contact	554	20	363	14
Other	26	1	30	1
Total	2,808	100	2,675	100

Table A1.4 Completion of self-completion questionnaire

	2000		2001
	Version A	Version B	Version A
Number of main stage interviews	895	905	1,800
Number of self-completions achieved	745	726	1,407
% of self-completions achieved	83	80	78

RESPONSE RATES

Table A1.3 shows the reason for non-achievement of interviews with adults drawn in the sample. Table A1.4 shows the response rate for versions A and B of the main stage interviews, as well as for the self-completion questionnaires.

SAMPLING ERRORS AND CONFIDENCE INTERVALS

Since no sample ever entirely represents the characteristics of the population from which it is drawn, it is necessary to estimate the amount of error due to the sampling methodology. The Life and Times survey uses a simple random sample design, whereby each member of the population has an equal chance of being included in the sample. For such a design, the sampling error of any percentage (p) can be calculated using the following formula, where n is the number of respondents upon which p is formulated:

$$Sampling\ error\ (s.e.)\ of\ p\ = \sqrt{p(100 - p)/n}$$

The 95 per cent confidence interval for the population percentage can be calculated, using the following formula:

$$95\ per\ cent\ confidence\ interval = p \pm 1.96 \times s.e.(p)$$

Table A1.5 displays the sampling errors and confidence intervals for key variables from the 2000 and 2001 Life and Times surveys. The margin of error for all sample estimates is within the parameters of ± 3%.

DATA PREPARATION

Data from the main stage of the survey were collected by CAPI using Surveycraft software. These were then converted to SPSS format to facilitate analysis. All paper-based data (self-completion questionnaires) were entered via the SPSS data entry system. The data files from the CAPI and self-completion questionnaires were then merged and were subject to an extensive range of inter- and intra-variable logic checks.

Occupational variables were derived using the Computer Assisted Standard Occupational Coding (CASOC) software. This programme enables a match to be made between the text describing the respondent's occupation and the most similar occupational description taken from the Registrar General's Standard Classification of Occupations. When a match is made, the system automatically assigns the official three digit code from the Standard Classification of Occupations to this case. This three digit code is the direct basis for the derivation of related information on a social class grouping.

DISSEMINATION

Survey results are put on the Life and Times web site <http://www.ark.ac.uk/nilt> six months after the end of fieldwork, providing frequency tables for every question, along with a breakdown by age, gender and religion. Users can also download the actual SPSS data files from the web site if they wish to undertake their own secondary analysis. Technical reports are produced for each year in Portable Document Format (PDF) and are posted at <http://www.ark.ac.uk/nilt/datasets/technotes.html>. The web site also includes publications and online resources relevant to the survey topics.

The datasets for each year are also lodged with the UK Data Archive at the University of Essex <http://www.data-archive.ac.uk>. Data relating to the ISSP module are lodged in the Zentralarchiv für Empirische Sozialforschung (Central Archive for Empirical Social Research) at the University of Cologne <http://www.gesis.org/en/za/index.htm>.

The survey team has also set up a helpline for those who need additional tables or have any query about the survey. A leaflet advertising the existence of the data and how to access them is also sent to schools, voluntary groups, civil servants, journalists and assembly members. The funders of the survey receive the dataset somewhat earlier than the public (three months after the end of fieldwork). However, funders also agree to one of the guiding principles of the survey, that the information is made available to all and that no one person or organisation has ownership of the results.

COMPARISON WITH OTHER SURVEYS

Another issue pertinent to social surveys is that of non-response bias, whereby the characteristics of non-respondents differ from those of respondents. In order to estimate non-response bias, the characteristics of the sample are compared with the same variables in the population at the time of sampling. The publication of key statistics from the 2001 Census of Population provides an opportunity for comparison with the Life and Times demographic characteristics, as shown in Tables A1.6 to A1.8.

Table A1.5 Sampling errors and confidence intervals for key variables by year

		% (p)	Standard error of p (%)	95% confidence intervals
2000	*Age*			
	18–24	10.2	0.71	8.80–11.60
	25–44	37.1	1.14	34.87–39.33
	45–64	30.4	1.08	28.27–32.53
	65–74	12.1	0.77	10.59–13.61
	75 years and over	10.1	0.71	8.71–11.46
	Gender			
	Male	42.9	1.17	40.61–45.19
	Female	57.1	1.17	54.81–59.39
	Marital status			
	Married/cohabiting	48.1	1.18	45.79–50.41
	Single	25.5	1.03	23.49–27.51
	Widowed/divorced/ separated	26.3	1.14	24.27–28.33
	Religion			
	Catholic	30.3	1.08	28.18–32.42
	Protestant	55.6	1.17	53.30–57.90
	No religion	10.5	0.72	9.08–11.92
	Other	2.6	0.38	1.86–3.34
	Refused	0.7	0.20	0.31–1.09
2001	*Age*			
	18–24	8.4	0.65	7.12–9.68
	25–44	38.2	1.15	35.96–40.44
	45–64	30.4	1.08	28.27–32.53
	65–74	13.0	0.79	11.45–14.55
	75 years and over	10.1	0.71	8.71–11.49
	Gender			
	Male	39.1	1.15	36.84–41.35
	Female	60.9	1.15	58.65–63.15
	Marital status			
	Married/co-habiting	52.8	1.18	50.49–55.11
	Single	24.8	1.02	22.80–26.80
	Widowed/divorced/ separated	22.2	0.98	20.28–24.12
	Religion			
	Catholic	37.7	1.14	35.46–39.94
	Protestant	46.1	1.17	43.80–48.40
	No religion	9.9	0.70	8.52–11.28
	Other	4.4	0.48	3.45–5.35
	Refused	1.9	0.32	1.27–2.53

Table A1.6   Comparison of household tenure (%)

	Life and Times 2000*	Life and Times 2001*	Census 2001
Owner occupied	64	64	70
Rented, NIHE	26	27	19
Rented, other**	8	7	9
Other (e.g. rent free)	1	1	2
Base	1,800	1,800	626,718

* household characteristics are based on unweighted data from the Life and Times survey
** 'Rented, other' includes rented from a housing association and rented privately

Table A1.7   Comparison of individual characteristics (%)

	Life and Times 2000	Life and Times 2001	Census 2001
Sex			
Male	45	41	48
Female	55	59	52
Age			
18–24	13	10	13
25–34	17	17	20
35–44	19	20	20
45–54	18	19	16
55–59	9	9	7
60–64	7	8	6
65 years and over	17	18	18
Base	1,800	1,800	1,233,753
Economic activity			
Working	50	48	58*
Unemployed	5	5	4
Economically inactive	45	47	38
Base	1,619	1,603	1,187,079

* based on respondents aged 18–74 inclusive

Table A1.8   Comparison of stated religious denomination (%)

	Life and Times 2000	Life and Times 2001	Census 2001
Protestant	57	47	48
Catholic	32	41	38
Other religion	<1	<1	<1
No religion	1	10	13*
Unwilling to say/ don't know	1	2	
Base	1,800	1,800	1,233751

* includes no religion and those refusing

REFERENCES

Breen, R., Devine, P. and Dowds, L. (eds) (1996) *Social Attitudes in Northern Ireland: The Fifth Report, 1995–1996* (Belfast: Appletree Press).

Breen, R., Devine, P. and Robinson, G. (eds) (1995) *Social Attitudes in Northern Ireland: The Fourth Report, 1994–1995* (Belfast: Appletree Press).

Dowds, L., Devine, P. and Breen, R. (eds) (1997) *Social Attitudes in Northern Ireland: The Sixth Report, 1996–1997* (Belfast: Appletree Press).

Gray, A.M., Lloyd, K., Devine P., Robinson, G. and Heenan, D. (eds) (2002) *Social Attitudes in Northern Ireland: The Eighth Report* (London: Pluto Press).

Robinson, G., Heenan, D., Gray, A.M. and Thompson, K. (eds) (1998) *Social Attitudes in Northern Ireland: The Seventh Report* (Aldershot: Ashgate).

Stringer, P. and Robinson, G. (eds) (1991) *Social Attitudes in Northern Ireland, 1990–91 Edition* (Belfast: Blackstaff Press).

Stringer, P. and Robinson, G. (eds) (1992) *Social Attitudes in Northern Ireland: The Second Report, 1991–92* (Belfast: Blackstaff Press).

Stringer, P. and Robinson, G. (eds) (1993) *Social Attitudes in Northern Ireland: The Third Report, 1992–1993* (Belfast: Blackstaff Press).

Appendix II
Notes on the Tabulations

1 Figures in the tables are from the 2000 or 2001 Northern Ireland Life and Times survey, unless otherwise indicated.
2 Tables are percentaged as indicated.
3 In tables, '<1' indicates less than 0.5 per cent, but greater than zero and – indicates zero.
4 When findings based on the responses of fewer than 100 respondents are reported in the text, reference is generally made to the small base size.
5 Percentages equal to or greater than 0.5 have been rounded up in all tables (for example, 0.5 per cent = 1 per cent, 36.5 per cent = 37 per cent).
6 In many tables the proportions of respondents answering 'don't know' or not giving an answer are omitted. This, together with the effects of rounding and weighting, means that percentages will not always add to 100 per cent.
7 The self-completion questionnaire was not completed by all respondents to the main questionnaire (see Appendix I). Percentage responses to the self-completion question-naire are based on all those who completed it.

Appendix III
Using Life and Times Survey Data

Tables of results for every question asked within the 2000 and 2001 Northern Ireland Life and Times surveys are available on the Life and Times survey web site <http://www.ark.ac.uk/nilt>. Results are available in the form of a frequency table, as well as cross-tabulations by age, sex and religious grouping (Catholic, Protestant and no religion).

While this book provides in-depth analysis on a variety of topics, and basic tables of results can be found on the web site, users may wish to undertake their own analysis of the data. For this reason, datasets are available from the Life and Times survey web site in SPSS portable file format. These can be downloaded and used for secondary analysis. The datasets are also deposited, and can be obtained from the UK Data Archive at the University of Essex <http://www.data-archive.ac.uk>. Datasets for all years of the Northern Ireland Social Attitudes survey, which ran from 1989 to 1996, are also deposited at the UK Data Archive. Data for modules included as part of the International Social Survey Programme (ISSP) are deposited at the Central Archive for Empirical Social Research at the University of Cologne <http://www.gesis.org/en/za/index.htm>.

Each year, the Life and Times survey includes modules on Political Attitudes and Community Relations, as well as background classificatory variables (for example, age, gender and housing tenure).

The following table identifies the topics included in all years of the Northern Ireland Social Attitudes survey, as well as the Life and Times survey, and indicates which topics were asked as part of the International Social Survey Programme.

Table A3.1 Topics by year of survey

	Northern Ireland Social Attitudes survey							Life and Times survey				
	1989	1990	1991	1993	1994	1995	1996	1998	1999	2000	2001	2002
Aids	✓											
Charitable giving			✓	✓								
Childcare				✓	✓							
Civil liberties		✓			✓		✓					
Constitutional issues	✓	✓	✓	✓	✓		✓	✓		✓	✓	
Countryside and the environment		✓		ISSP	✓		✓		✓	ISSP		✓
Crime	✓	✓					✓	✓				✓
Culture, arts and leisure		✓										
Defence	✓	✓										
Devolution			✓					✓	✓	✓	✓	
Diet and health	✓		✓									
Drugs						✓						
Economic activity	✓	✓	✓	✓	✓	✓	✓	✓	✓	✓	✓	✓
Economic issues and policies	✓	✓	✓	✓	✓	✓	✓	✓	✓	✓	✓	✓
Education	✓	✓	✓	✓	✓	✓		✓	✓			
European Community	✓	✓	✓	✓	✓	✓	✓	✓	✓		✓	✓
Even-handedness of institutions	✓	✓	✓	✓	✓	✓		✓				
Even-handedness of security forces	✓	✓	✓	✓	✓	✓		✓				
Family networks											ISSP	
Gender issues at the workplace			✓		✓							

Topic											
Gender roles							ISSP		✓	✓	✓ ISSP
Genetics research										✓	
Health care	✓	✓	✓	✓ ISSP	✓	✓	✓	✓	✓	✓	✓
Household income	✓	✓	✓	✓	✓	✓	✓	✓	✓	✓	✓
Housing	✓		✓	✓	✓						
Informal carers	✓	✓	✓	✓	✓	✓	✓	✓	✓	✓	✓
Integrated education			✓	✓	✓	✓					
International relations	✓			✓							
Men's Life and Times	✓										
Moral issues	✓	✓	✓	✓	✓	✓	✓	✓	✓	✓	✓
National identity	✓	✓	✓	✓ ISSP	✓	✓	✓	✓	✓	✓	✓
Newspaper readership	✓	✓	✓	✓	✓	✓	✓	✓	✓	✓	✓
Northern Ireland Assembly							✓	✓	✓	✓	✓
Peace process									✓	✓	✓
Pensions and pensioners	✓	✓	✓	✓							
Police	✓	✓	✓	✓	✓		✓	✓	✓	✓	✓
Political partisanship	✓	✓	✓	✓	✓	✓	✓	✓	✓	✓	✓
Political trust	✓	✓	✓				✓	✓	✓	✓	✓
Poverty	✓	✓	✓	✓	✓		✓	✓	✓	✓	✓
Protestant–Catholic relations	✓						✓	✓	✓	✓	✓
Public understanding of science											
Race and immigration	✓		✓	✓	✓	✓	✓	✓	✓	✓	✓

Table A3.1 (continued)

	Northern Ireland Social Attitudes survey							Life and Times survey				
	1989	1990	1991	1993	1994	1995	1996	1998	1999	2000	2001	2002
Religious beliefs			✓ ISSP					✓ ISSP				
Religious denomination and attendance	✓	✓	✓	✓	✓	✓	✓	✓	✓	✓	✓	✓
Religious prejudice and discrimination	✓	✓	✓	✓	✓	✓	✓	✓	✓	✓	✓	✓
Rights of the child								✓				
Role of government		✓ ISSP					✓ ISSP					
Security operations												
Segregation and integration		✓	✓	✓		✓	✓	✓	✓	✓	✓	✓
Single parenthood and child support					✓							
Social capital										✓		
Social class	✓	✓		✓								
Social inequality									✓ ISSP			
Taxation and public spending	✓	✓	✓	✓	✓	✓	✓	✓	✓	✓	✓	✓
Trade union activity	✓	✓	✓	✓	✓	✓	✓	✓	✓	✓	✓	✓
Transport					✓	✓			✓			
Troop withdrawal	✓	✓	✓	✓	✓		✓					
Trust in public institutions	✓			✓	✓		✓	✓	✓	✓	✓	✓
Welfare reform										✓		
Welfare state	✓	✓	✓	✓	✓	✓	✓	✓	✓			
Women in politics										✓		✓
Work orientations	✓ ISSP											

Contributors

Boyd Black
Senior Lecturer, School of Management and Economics, Queen's University Belfast

Mary Daly
Professor, School of Sociology and Social Policy, Queen's University Belfast

Paula Devine
Research Director of ARK (Northern Ireland Social and Political Archive), Institute of Governance, Public Policy and Social Research, Queen's University Belfast

John Field
Director, Division of Academic Innovation and Continuing Education, University of Stirling

Colin Fowler
Regional Manager, The Men's Project, Parents' Advice Centre, Northern Ireland

Ann Marie Gray
Lecturer, School of Policy Studies, University of Ulster and Policy Director of ARK

Jeremy Harbison
Senior Fellow, Institute of Governance, Public Policy and Social Research, Queen's University Belfast

Deirdre Heenan
Senior Lecturer, School of Policy Studies, University of Ulster

Katrina Lloyd
Research Director of ARK, Institute of Governance, Public Policy and Social Research, Queen's University Belfast

Anna Manwah Lo
Chief Executive, Chinese Welfare Association, Northern Ireland

Roger MacGinty
Lecturer, Department of Politics, University of York

Kate Thompson
Research Officer, School of Nursing, University of Ulster

Dorothy Whittington
Director of Education, Research and Development, North Bristol NHS Trust

Index